AF255950

MY CROCKPOT GUIDE

2022

TASTY RECIPES EASY TO MAKE FOR BEGINNERS

STEPHANIE LOHAN

Table of Contents

Geoff's Easy Roast Chicken with Gravy

INGREDIENTS

- 1 chicken, roaster

- salt and pepper

PREPARATION

1.
We simply clean out the chicken, give it a wash then pop it in the crockpot. Add a pinch of salt and a sprinkle of pepper. Leave for about 6 hours on high.

2.
When we take the finished product out we drain the remaining juice into a mug, cover with foil and put it in the freezer for about half an hour. This solidifies all the fat at the top of the mug. Scrape this off and the stock that's left we add to the gravy.

Gingered Pineapple Chicken

INGREDIENTS

- 4 to 5 boneless chicken breast halves, cubed (about 3/4-inch)

- 1 bunch green onions, with about 3 inches of green sliced 1/2-inch

- 1 can (8oz) crushed pineapple, undrained

- 1 tablespoon finely chopped crystallized ginger

- 2 tablespoons lemon juice

- 2 tablespoons soy sauce (low sodium)

- 3 tablespoons brown sugar or honey

- 1/2 teaspoon garlic powder

PREPARATION

1.
Combine all ingredients in the slow cooker; cover and cook on low for 6 to 8 hours. Serve over rice or flat noodles.

2.
Serves 4.

Greek Chicken

INGREDIENTS

-

4 to 6 skinless chicken breasts

-

1 lg. can (15 ounces) tomato sauce

-

1 can (14.5 ounces) diced tomatoes with juice

-

1 can sliced mushrooms

-

1 can (4 ounces) sliced ripe olives

-

2 cloves garlic, minced

-

1 tbsp. lemon juice

-

1 tsp. dried leaf oregano

-

1/2 cup chopped onion

-

1/2 c. dry white wine (optional)

-

2 cups hot cooked rice

•

Salt to taste

PREPARATION

1.

Wash chicken and pat dry. Bake in 350° oven for about 30 minutes. Meanwhile, combine all other ingredients (except rice). Dice chicken and combine with the sauce; cover and cook on low for 4 to 5 hours. Serve chicken and sauce with hot cooked rice.

2.

Serves 4 to 6.

Hawaiian Drumsticks

INGREDIENTS

- 12 chicken drumsticks

- 1 cup ketchup

- 1 cup packed dark brown sugar

- 1/2 cup soy sauce

- grated fresh ginger, 1 tablespoon

- a splash of sesame seed oil

PREPARATION

1.
Cover and crock on low for about 8 hours. Serve on top of white rice.

2.
Aloha!

3.
Chicken drumsticks recipe shared by LeRoy and the Nitz Dawg!

Herbed Chicken With Vegetables

INGREDIENTS

- 3 to 4 pounds chicken pieces

- 1 1/2 to 2 cups frozen or canned and drained small whole onions

- 2 cups whole baby carrots

- 2 medium potatoes, cut in 1-inch chunks

- 1 1/2 cups chicken broth

- 2 medium celery ribs, cut in 2-inch chunks

- 2 slices bacon, diced

- 1 bay leaf

- 1/4 teaspoon dried thyme

- 1/4 teaspoon black pepper

- 1/4 cup minced fresh parsley

- 2 tablespoons fresh tarragon, minced, or 1 teaspoon dried tarragon

- 1 teaspoon grated lemon peel

- 2 tablespoons fresh lemon juice

- 1/2 teaspoon salt, or to taste

PREPARATION

1.

In slow cooker, combine chicken, onions, carrots, potatoes, broth, celery, bacon, bay leaf, thyme and pepper. Set on low and cook 8 to 10 hours.

2.

Set aside.

3.

Remove chicken and vegetables to heated platter, using a slotted spoon. Cover with foil and keep warm. Skim off and discard excess fat. Stir in the parsley, tarragon, lemon zest and lemon juice, along with salt to taste; spoon over chicken and vegetables.

Herbed Chicken with Wild Rice

INGREDIENTS

- 1 to 1 1/2 pound chicken tenders or boneless chicken breast halves

- 6 to 8 ounces sliced mushrooms

- 1 tablespoon vegetable oil

- 2 to 3 slices crumbled bacon, or 2 tablespoons real bacon bits

- 1 teaspoon butter

- 1 (6 oz.) box Uncle Bens (chicken flavor) long grain and wild rice

- 1 can cream of of chicken soup, with herbs or plain

- 1 cup water

- 1 teaspoon herb mixture, such as fine herbes or a mixture of your favorites; parsley, thyme, tarragon, etc.

PREPARATION

1.

Saute chicken pieces and mushrooms in oil and butter until chicken is lightly browned. Place bacon on bottom of 3 1/2 to 5-quart slow cooker. Place rice over bacon. Reserve package of seasonings. Place chicken tenders over rice - if using chicken breasts, cut in strips or cubes. Pour soup over chicken, then add water. Top with seasonings and sprinkle with herb mixture. Cover and cook on LOW for 5 1/2 to 6 1/2 hours, or until rice is tender (not mushy).

2.

Serves 4 to 6.

Honey and Ginger Chicken

INGREDIENTS

- 3 pounds chicken breast halves without skin

- 1 1/4 inch fresh ginger root, peeledand finely chopped

- 2 cloves garlic, minced

- 1/2 cup soy sauce

- 1/2 cup honey

- 3 tablespoons dry sherry

- 2 tablespoons cornstarch blended with 2 tablespoons water

PREPARATION

1.

Combine ginger, garlic, soy sauce, honey, and sherry in a small bowl. Dip chicken pieces into sauce; place chicken pieces in slow cooker; pour remaining sauce over all. Cover and cook on LOW for about 6 hours.

2.

Remove chicken to warm serving dish and pour the liquids into a saute pan or skillet. Bring to a boil and continue simmering for 3 to 4 minutes to reduce slightly. Whisk the cornstarch into the sauce mixture.

3.

Cook over low heat until thickened. Pour a little sauce over chicken and pass remainder.

4.

Serve chicken with hot rice.

Honey Barbecued Chicken with Sweet Potatoes

INGREDIENTS

- 3 cups peeled and sliced sweet potatoes, about 2 medium to large sweet potatoes

- 1 can (8 ounces) pineapple chunks in juice, undrained

- 1/2 cup chicken broth

- 1/4 cup finely chopped onion

- 1/2 teaspoon ground ginger

- 1/3 cup barbecue sauce, your favorite

- 2 tablespoons honey

- 1/2 teaspoon dry mustard

- 4 to 6 chicken leg quarters (legs with thighs, skin removed

PREPARATION

1.
In 3 1/2 to 5-quart slow cooker, combine sweet potatoes, pineapple with juice, chicken broth, chopped onion, and ground ginger; stir to blend well. In small bowl, combine barbecue sauce, honey, and dry mustard; stir to blend well. Coat chicken generously on all sides barbecue sauce mixture. Arrange coated chicken in single layer over sweet potato and pineapple mixture, overlapping if necessary. Spoon any remaining barbecue sauce mixture over chicken.

2.
Cover; cook on low setting for 7 to 9 hours or until chicken is fork tender and juices run clear, and sweet potatoes are tender.

3.
Serves 4 to 6.

Honey Hoisin Chicken

INGREDIENTS

-

2 to 3 lbs chicken parts (or whole chicken, cut up)

-

2 tablespoons soy sauce

-

2 tablespoons hoisin sauce

-

2 tablespoons honey

-

2 tablespoons dry white wine

-

1 tablespoon grated ginger root or 1 teaspoon ground ginger

-

1/8 teaspoon ground black pepper

-

2 tablespoons cornstarch

-

2 tablespoons water

PREPARATION

1.

Wash chicken and pat dry; arrange in bottom of slow cooker.

2.

Combine soy sauce, hoisin sauce, honey, wine, ginger and pepper. Pour sauce over chicken.

3.

Cover and cook on low about 5 1/2 to 8 hours, or until chicken is tender and juices run clear.

4.

Mix cornstarch and water.

5.

Remove chicken from slow cooker; turn on high and add cornstarch and water mixture.

6.

Continue to cook until thickened, and add chicken back to slow cooker to heat through.

Italian Style Chicken

INGREDIENTS

- 4 chicken breasts, boneless, cut into bite size pieces

- 1 - 16 oz. can of tomatoes, chopped

- 1 large green sweet pepper, diced

- 1 small cooking onion, diced

- 1 medium rib of celery, diced

- 1 medium carrot, peeled and diced

- 1 bay leaf

- 1 teaspoon dried oregano

- 1 teaspoon dried basil

- 1/2 teaspoon dried thyme, optional

- 2 cloves of garlic, chopped; OR 2 tsp. garlic powder

- 1/2 teaspoon salt

- 1/2 teaspoon red pepper flakes, or to taste

- 1/2 cup grated Parmesan or Romano cheese

PREPARATION

1.

Combine all ingredients, except grated cheese, in slow cooker.

2.

Cover and cook on low for 6 to 8 hours. Remove bay leaf and sprinkle with grated cheese before serving.

3.

Good over rice or pasta.

Italian Style Chicken in the Crockpot
INGREDIENTS

-

1 pound boneless chicken thighs, skin removed, or 4 chicken leg quarters, skin removed

-

1/2 cup chopped onion

-

1/2 cup sliced pitted ripe olives

-

1 can (14.5-ounce) diced tomatoes, undrained

-

1 teaspoon dried leaf oregano

-

1/2 teaspoon salt

-

1/2 teaspoon dried rosemary, crumbled

-

pinch dried leaf thyme

-

1/4 teaspoon garlic powder

-

1/4 cup cold water or chicken broth

-

1 tablespoon cornstarch

PREPARATION

1.

Place chicken in 3 1/2 to 5-quart slow cooker. Top with chopped onion and sliced olives. Combine tomatoes with oregano, salt, rosemary, thyme, and garlic powder. Pour tomato mixture over chicken. Cover and cook on LOW for 7 to 9 hours, or until chicken is fork tender and juices run clear. With slotted spoon, remove chicken and vegetables to a warm serving platter. Cover with foil and keep warm. Increase crockpot to HIGH.

2.

In cup or small bowl, combine water or broth and cornstarch; stir until smooth. Stir into liquids in the crockpot. Cover and cook until thickened. Serve thickened sauce with chicken.

3.

Serves 4.

Italian Style Chicken With Spaghetti, Slow Cooker

INGREDIENTS

-

1 can (8 ounces) tomato sauce

-

6 to 8 boneless chicken breast halves, skin removed

-

1 can (6 ounces) tomato paste

-

3 tablespoons water

-

3 medium cloves garlic, minced

-

2 teaspoons dried leaf oregano, crushed

-

1 teaspoon sugar, or to taste

-

hot cooked spaghetti

-

4 ounces shredded mozzarella cheese

-

grated Parmesan cheese

PREPARATION

1. If desired, brown the chicken in hot oil; drain. Sprinkle generously with salt and pepper. Arrange chicken in slow cooker. Combine tomato sauce, tomato paste, water, garlic, oregano and sugar; pour over the chicken. Cover and cook on LOW for 6 to 8 hours. Remove chicken and keep warm. Turn cooker to high heat setting, stir mozzarella cheese into sauce. Cook uncovered, till cheese melts and sauce is heated through.
2. Serve chicken and sauce over hot cooked spaghetti. Serve with Parmesan cheese.
3. Serves 6 to 8.

Light Chicken Stroganoff

INGREDIENTS

-

1 cup fat-free sour cream

-

1 tablespoon Gold Metal all-purpose flour

-

1 envelope chicken gravy mix (approximately 1 ounce)

-

1 cup water

-

1 pound boneless skinless chicken breast, cut into 1-inch pieces

-

16 ounces frozen California blend vegetables, thawed

-

1 cup sliced mushroom, sauteed

-

1 cup frozen peas

-

10 ounces potatoes, peeled and cut into 1-inch pieces, about 2 medium peeled potatoes

-

1 1/2 cups Bisquick baking mix

-

4 green onions, chopped (1/3 cups)

-

1/2 cup 1% low-fat milk

PREPARATION

1. Mix sour cream, flour, gravy mix and water in 3-1/2 to 5-quart crockpot until smooth. Stir in chicken, vegetables and mushrooms. Cover and cook on low heat setting 4 hours or until chicken in tender and sauce is thickened. Stir in peas. Mix baking mix and onions. Stir in milk just until moistened. Drop dough by rounded tablespoonfuls onto chicken-vegetables mixtures. Cover and cook on high heat setting 45 to 50 minutes or until toothpick inserted in center of dumplings coming out clean.
2. Serve immediately 4 Servings.

Lilly's Slow Cooker Chicken With Cheese Sauce

INGREDIENTS

- 6 boneless, skinless chicken breast halves

- 2 cans cream of chicken soup

- 1 can cheese soup

- salt, pepper, garlic powder to taste

PREPARATION

1. Sprinkle chicken breasts with garlic powder, salt, and pepper.
2. Place 3 chicken breasts in slow cooker. Combine all soups; pour half of the soup over the first 3 chicken breasts.
3. Place the remaining 3 chicken breasts on top. Pour remaining soup over the top.
4. Cover and cook on LOW for 6 to 8 hours.

Mexican-Style Chicken Breasts

INGREDIENTS

- 2 tablespoons vegetable oil

- 3 to 4 boneless chicken breast halves, without skin, cut into 1-inch pieces

- 1/2 cup chopped onion

- 1 green bell pepper (or use a red bell pepper)

- 1 to 2 small jalapeno peppers, finely chopped

- 3 cloves garlic, minced

- 1 can (4 ounces) mild chile peppers, chopped

- 1 can (14 1/2 ounce) Mexican style, chili style, or fire-roasted diced tomatoes

- 1 teaspoon dried leaf oregano

- 1/4 teaspoon ground cumin

- shredded Mexican blend cheese

- salsa

-

Optional Garnishes

-

sour cream

-

guacamole

-

sliced green onions

-

diced tomatoes

-

shredded lettuce

-

sliced ripe olives

-

cilantro

PREPARATION

1. Heat oil in a large skillet over medium heat. Brown chicken breasts. Remove and drain.
2. In the same skillet, sauté onion, green bell pepper, garlic and jalapeno pepper just until tender.
3. Put the chicken breasts and onion mixture in the slow cooker.
4. Add mild chile peppers, tomatoes, oregano, and cumin to the slow cooker; stir to combine.

5. Cover and cook on LOW 6 to 8 hours (HIGH 3 to 4 hours).
6. Serve with warm flour tortillas, shredded cheese, and salsa, along with your favorite toppings and condiments.
7. Guacamole or sour cream would make a nice garnish with sliced green onions or diced tomatoes.

Paula's Chicken With Leeks

INGREDIENTS

- 3 to 4 pounds chicken parts, bone-in

- 4 to 6 potatoes, sliced about 1/4-inch thick

- 1 package leek soup mix

- 1 thinly sliced leek or 4 sliced green onions

- 1/2 to 1 cup water

- paprika

- Seasonings •

PREPARATION

1. Layer potatoes in bottom of slow cooker/Crock Pot, top with onion or leek, and then add chicken. (If you will have several layers of chicken, salt and pepper bottom layers as you put them in. Don't season top layer yet.) Mix leek soup with approximately 1/2 cup water; pour over all. Season top layer of chicken. At this point, I also sprinkle with paprika to give it color.

• If you like, add minced garlic and some fresh rosemary to season.

Cook on low for 6 to 7 hours, adding more water if needed.

Saucy Jack Daniel's Barbecue Chicken Drumettes

INGREDIENTS

- 5 to 6 pounds chicken drumettes

- 1 cup all-purpose flour

- 1 teaspoon salt

- 1/2 teaspoon ground black pepper

-

Barbecue Sauce

- 1 1/2 cups ketchup

- 4 tablespoons butter

- 1/2 cup Jack Daniels or other good quality whisky

- 5 tablespoons brown sugar

- 3 tablespoons molasses

- 3 tablespoons cider vinegar

-

2 tablespoons Worcestershire sauce

-

1 tablespoon soy sauce

-

4 teaspoons Dijon style mustard or a gourmet mustard

-

2 teaspoons liquid smoke

-

1 1/2 teaspoons onion powder

-

1 teaspoon garlic powder

-

1 tablespoon sriracha, or more, to taste (may substitute about 1 scant teaspoon cayenne pepper)

-

1/2 teaspoon ground black pepper

PREPARATION

1. Line 2 rimmed baking sheets with foil; spray with nonstick cooking spray. Heat the oven to 425°.
2. Toss the drumettes with a mixture of the flour, 1 teaspoon of salt, and 1/2 teaspoon of pepper.
3. Arrange on the baking sheets and bake for 20 minutes. Turn the drumettes and return to the oven. Bake for 20 minutes longer, or until nicely browned.
4. Meanwhile, put all sauce ingredients in a medium saucepan; mix well and bring to a boil over medium heat.
5. Reduce heat and simmer for 5 minutes.
6. Transfer the drumettes to a bowl or slow cooker insert (if you'll be keeping them warm for a party). Toss with about half of the barbecue sauce. Serve immediately with the sauce or turn the slow cooker on LOW to keep them warm. If not serving immediately, refrigerate the remaining sauce until serving time.
7. Serve the drumettes hot with the sauce for dipping. Have plenty of napkins on hand.
8. This recipe makes about 3 dozen pieces, enough for 6 to 8 people as an appetizer..

Sherri's Chicken & Dumplings

INGREDIENTS

- 4 chicken breast halves

- 2 cans chicken broth (3 1/2 cups)

- 1 cup water

- 3 cubes chicken bouillon or equivalent base or granules

- 1 small carrot, chopped

- 1 small rib celery, chopped

- 1/2 cup chopped onion

- 12 large flour tortillas

PREPARATION

1. Combine all ingredients in slow cooker, except tortillas. Cook on low 8 to 10 hours. Take out chicken and remove meat from bones, then place broth on stove in large pot. Cut chicken into bite-size pieces and return to broth on stovetop. Bring to a slow boil.
2. Cut tortillas in half, then in 1-inch strips. Place strips into simmering broth and boil gently for 15 to 20 minutes, stir occasionally. Broth should thicken but if too thin, combine 1 tablespoon cornstarch with just enough water to dissolve and stir into broth.
3. Cook 5 to 10 minutes more.
4. Serves 4.

Simple Slow Cooker Chicken Barbecue

INGREDIENTS

- 3 boneless chicken breast halves

- 1 1/2 cups spicy barbecue sauce, your choice, plus more for serving

- 1 medium onion, sliced or chopped

- toasted buns

- coleslaw, for serving

PREPARATION

1. Wash the chicken breasts and pat dry. Put in a slow cooker with 1 1/2 cups of barbecue sauce and the onion. Stir to coat the chicken. Cover and cook on HIGH for 3 hours.
2. Remove the chicken breasts to a plate and shred or chop. Return the shredded chicken to the sauce in the slow cooker; stir to blend. Cover and cook for 10 minutes longer.
3. Serve the shredded chicken on toasted buns with coleslaw and extra barbecue sauce.
4. Serves 4 to 6.

Slow-Cooked Chicken Dijon

INGREDIENTS

- 1 to 2 pounds chicken breast tenders

- 1 can condensed cream of chicken soup, undiluted (10 1/2 ounce)

- 2 tablespoons regular or grainy Dijon mustard

- 1 tablespoon cornstarch

- 1/2 cup water

- pepper to taste

- 1 teaspoon dried parsley flakes or 1 tablespoon fresh chopped parsley

PREPARATION

1. Wash chicken and pat dry; arrange in the slow cooker. Combine the soup with mustard and cornstar; add water and stir. Stir in parsley and pepper. Pour the mixture over the chicken. Cover and cook on LOW for 6 to 7 hours. Serve with hot cooked rice and a side vegetable.
2. Chicken Dijon recipe serves 4 to 6.

Slow Cooker Barbecue Chicken

INGREDIENTS

*

3 to 4 pounds chicken pieces

*

1 large onion, coarsely chopped

*

1 bottle barbecue sauce

PREPARATION

1. Put chicken in bottom of slow cooker or crockpot and add onions and barbecue sauce. Cook on LOW for about 6 to 8 hours, or until chicken is tender but not falling apart.
2. Serves 4 to 6.

Slow Cooker Barbecued Chicken Thighs

INGREDIENTS

- 1/2 cup flour

- 1/2 teaspoon garlic powder

- 1 teaspoon dry mustard

- 1 teaspoon salt

- 1/4 teaspoon pepper

- 8 chicken thighs

- 2 tablespoons vegetable oil

- 1 cup thick barbecue sauce

PREPARATION

1. Put flour, garlic powder, mustard, salt, and pepper in a food storage bag. Add chicken, a few pieces at a time, and shake to coat thoroughly. Heat oil in large skillet; add chicken and brown on all sides. Put half of the barbecue sauce in crockpot; add chicken then add remaining sauce. Cook on low 6 to 7 hours, or until chicken is tender and juices run clear.
2. Serves 4 to 6.

Slow Cooker Chicken and Sausage Pasta Sauce

INGREDIENTS

- 1 tablespoon olive oil

- 4 garlic cloves, crushed

- 1/2 cup chopped onion

- 1 red bell pepper, chopped

- 1 green bell pepper, chopped

- 1 small zucchini, chopped

- 1 can (4 ounces) mushrooms

- 1 can stewed tomatoes, Italian seasoned

- 1 can (6 ounces) tomato paste

- 3 sweet Italian sausage links

- 4 boneless chicken breast halves, cut in strips

- 1 teaspoon Italian seasoning

•

red pepper flakes, to taste, optional

PREPARATION

1. Heat oil in skillet. Saute onion and garlic until light brown. Remove.
2. Add sausage; brown on all sides. Add chicken and cook just until browned. Drain off excess fat. Slice sausages in 1-inch pieces. In slow cooker combine all remaining ingredients with the onions and garlic. Add the sausage then top with the chicken strips. Cover and cook on LOW 4 to 6 hours, until chicken is tender but not dry.
3. Serve this tasty sauce over hot cooked pasta.
4. Serves 4.

Slow Cooker Chicken Curry

INGREDIENTS

- 2 whole chicken breasts, boned and diced

- 1 can cream of chicken soup

- 1/4 cup dry sherry

- 2 tbsp. butter or margarine

- 2 green onions with tops, finely chopped

- 1/4 tsp. curry powder

- 1 tsp. salt

- Dash of pepper

- hot cooked rice

PREPARATION

1. Place chicken in crockpot. Add all remaining ingredients, except rice. Cover and cook on Low for 4 to 6 hours, or on HIGH 2 to 3 hours. Serve over hot rice.

Slow Cooker Chicken Curry With Rice

INGREDIENTS

- 4 boneless, skinless chicken breasts, cut in 1 inch strips or chunks

- 2 large onions, quartered and sliced thinly

- 3 cloves garlic, minced

- 1 tablespoon soy sauce or Tamari

- 1 teaspoon Madras curry powder

- 2 teaspoons chili powder

- 1 teaspoon turmeric

- 1 teaspoon ground ginger

- 1/3 cup chicken broth or water

- salt and freshly ground black pepper, to taste

- hot cooked rice

PREPARATION

1. Mix all ingredients, except rice, together in the slow cooker or /Crock Pot.
2. Cover and cook on low from 6 to 8 hours, or until chicken is tender.
3. Taste and season with salt and pepper, as needed.
4. Serve over rice or noodles

Slow Cooker Chicken Enchiladas

INGREDIENTS

- 3 cups diced cooked chicken

- 3 cups shredded Mexican blend cheese with peppers, divided

- 1 can (4.5 ounces) chopped green chile peppers

- 1/4 cup chopped fresh cilantro

- 1 1/2 cups sour cream, divided

- 8 flour tortillas (8 inch)

- 1 cup tomatillo salsa

- Suggested Garnishes: diced tomatoes, sliced green onions, ripe olives, jalapeno rings, chopped fresh cilantro

PREPARATION

1. Lightly grease the crockery insert of a 4- to 6-quart slow cooker.
2. In a bowl combine the diced chicken with 2 cups of the shredded cheese, chopped green chile peppers, 1/4 cup chopped cilantro, and 1/2 cup of sour cream; stir to blend ingredients.
3. Spoon some chicken mixture down the center of the tortillas, dividing mixture evenly among all eight tortillas. Roll them up and arrange, seam side down, in the prepared slow cooker.
4. If necessary, stack the tortillas.
5. In a small bowl, combine the salsa with the remaining 1 cup of sour cream. Spoon the mixture over the tortillas.
6. Cover and cook on LOW for 4 hours. Sprinkle the tortillas with the remaining shredded cheese. Cover and cook on LOW for about 20 to 30 minutes longer.
7. Serves 4 to 6.

Slow Cooker Chicken Fricassee With Vegetables

INGREDIENTS

- 4 to 6 boneless chicken breast halves, skin removed

- salt and pepper to taste

- 2 tablespoons butter

- 2 cloves garlic, minced

- 3 tablespoons all-purpose flour

- 2 cups low sodium chicken broth

- 1 teaspoon dried leaf thyme

- 1/2 teaspoon dried leaf tarragon

- 3 to 4 carrots, cut in 2-inch pieces

- 2 onions, halved, thickly sliced

- 2 large leeks, white part only, washed and chopped

- 1 bay leaf

-

1/2 cup half-and-half or light cream

-

1 1/2 cups frozen peas, thawed

PREPARATION

1. Wash chicken breasts and pat dry. Set aside. Saute minced garlic in butter for a minute, then add flour and cook, stirring, until smooth. Pour in broth (you can use 1/4 cup of dry white wine or sherry in place of some of the broth), the thyme and tarragon, and stir until thickened. Layer in the Crock Pot the onions, carrots, chicken, then leeks; pour sauce over all. Add bay leaf. Cover and cook on LOW for 6 to 7 hours, or on HIGH for 3 to 5 hours.
2. If cooking on low, change to high and stir in half and half and thawed peas. Cover and continue cooking on high another 15 minutes, or until peas are heated through. Taste and adjust seasonings. Remove bay leaf before serving.
3. Serves 4 to 6.

Slow Cooker Chicken in Spicy Sauce

INGREDIENTS

- 1/2 c. tomato juice

- 1/2 c. soy sauce

- 1/2 c. brown sugar

- 1/4 c. chicken broth

- 3 garlic cloves, minced

- 3 to 4 pounds chicken pieces, skin removed

PREPARATION

1. Combine all ingredients except chicken in a deep bowl. Dip each piece of chicken in the sauce. Place in the slow cooker. Pour remaining sauce over the top. Cook on low for 6 to 8 hours or high for 3 to 4 hours.
2. Makes 6 servings.

Slow Cooker Chicken Madras With Curry Powder

INGREDIENTS

- 3 onions, thinly sliced

- 4 apples, peeled, cored and thinly sliced

- 1 teaspoon salt

- 1 to 2 teaspoons curry powder, or to taste

- 1 frying chicken, cut up

- paprika

PREPARATION

1. In crockpot, combine onion and apples; sprinkle with salt and curry powder. Mix well. Arrange chicken skin down over onion mixture. sprinkle generously with paprika.
2. Cover and cook on LOW for 6 to 8 hours, until chicken is tender.
3. Taste and add more seasonings, if needed.
4. Serves 4.

Slow Cooker Chicken With Mushrooms

INGREDIENTS

- 6 bone-in chicken breast halves, skin removed

- 1 1/4 teaspoons salt

- 1/4 teaspoon pepper

- 1/4 teaspoon paprika

- 1 3/4 teaspoons chicken flavored bouillon granules or chicken base

- 1 1/2 cups sliced fresh mushrooms

- 1/2 cup green onions, sliced, with green

- 1/2 cup dry white wine

- 1/2 cup evaporated milk

- 5 teaspoons cornstarch

- fresh chopped parsley

PREPARATION

1. Wash chicken and pat dry. In a bowl, combine salt, pepper and paprika. Rub over all sides of chicken, using all of the mixture. In a slow cooker, alternate layers of chicken, bouillon granules or base, mushrooms and green onions. Pour wine slowly over top. Do not stir ingredients. Cover and cook on high for 2 1/2 to 3 hours or on low for 5 to 6 hours or until chicken is tender but not falling apart.

2. With a slotted spoon, remove chicken and vegetables to a serving platter or bowl. Cover with foil and keep chicken warm. In a small saucepan, combine evaporated milk and cornstarch, stirring until smooth. Gradually stir in 2 cups of the cooking liquid. Stirring over medium heat, bring to a boil; continue to boi for 1 minute, or until thickened. Spoon some of the sauce over chicken and garnish with parsley, if desired. Serve with hot cooked rice or noodles, if desired.

Slow Cooker Cordon Bleu

INGREDIENTS

- 6 chicken breast halves, boneless, skinless - pounded to flatten slightly

- 6 thin slices ham

- 6 thin slices Swiss cheese

- 1/4 to 1/2 cup flour, for coating

- 1/2 pound sliced mushrooms

- 1/2 cup chicken broth

- 1/2 cup dry white wine (or use chicken broth)

- 1/2 teaspoon rosemary, crushed

- 1/4 cup grated Parmesan cheese

- 2 teaspoons cornstarch mixed with 1 tablespoon cool water

- salt and pepper to taste

PREPARATION

1. Place a slice of ham and slice of cheese on each flattened chicken breast and roll up. Secure with toothpicks and roll each in flour to coat. Place mushrooms in the slow cooker, then the chicken breasts. Whisk together the broth, wine (if using), and rosemary; pour over chicken. Sprinkle with the Parmesan cheese. Cover and cook on low for 6 to 7 hours. Just before serving, remove the chicken; keep warm.
2. To juices in slow cooker, add cornstarch mixture; stir until thickened. Salt and pepper, then taste and adjust seasonings. Pour sauce over chicken rolls and serve.
3. Serves 6.

Slow Cooker Dijon Chicken

INGREDIENTS

- 4 boneless chicken breast halves

- 1 heaping tablespoon honey Dijon mustard

- salt and coarsely ground black pepper or seasoned pepper

- 2 packages (8 ounces each) baby spinach, or 1 pound washed and dried fresh spinach leaves

- 2 tablespoons butter, cut in small pieces

- chopped fresh cilantro or parsley, optional

- toasted sliced almonds, optional•

PREPARATION

1. Grease the crockery insert of the slow cooker or spray with nonstick cooking spray.
2. Wash chicken breasts and pat dry.
3. Rub the chicken with the honey mustard; sprinkle with salt and pepper.
4. Arrange the chicken breasts in the crockery insert of the slow cooker. Top with spinach.
5. If your slow cooker is too small for all of the spinach, steam it briefly and add the wilted spinach leaves.

6. Dot spinach with butter and sprinkle with more salt and pepper.
7.
8. Garnish with cilantro or parsley or sprinkle with toasted almonds before serving, if desired.
9. Cover and cook on LOW for 5 to 6 hours.

•To toast almonds, add to a dry skillet over medium heat. Cook, constantly stirring, until lightly browned and aromatic.

Slow Cooker Lemon Chicken

INGREDIENTS

- 1 broiler-fryer,cut up, or about 3 1/2 pounds chicken pieces

- 1 teaspoon crumbled dry leaf oregano

- 2 cloves garlic, minced

- 2 tablespoons butter

- 1/4 cup dry wine, sherry, chicken broth, or water

- 3 tablespoons lemon juice

- Salt and pepper

PREPARATION

1. Season the chicken pieces with salt and pepper. Sprinkle half of garlic and oregano over the chicken.
2. Melt butter in a sauté pan over medium heat and brown chicken on all sides.
3. Transfer chicken to crockpot. Sprinkle with remaining oregano and garlic. Add wine or sherry to the sauté pan and stir to loosen brown bits; pour into slow cooker.
4. Cover and cook on LOW (200°) for 7 to 8 hours. Add lemon juice last hour.
5. Skim fat from juices and pour to a serving bowl; thicken juices, if desired.
6. Serve chicken with juices.
7. Serves 4.

Slow Cooker Pulled Chicken

INGREDIENTS

- 1 tablespoon butter

- 1 cup chopped onions

- 1/2 teaspoon minced garlic

- 1 1/2 cups tomato ketchup

- 1/2 cup apricot preserves, or peach preserves

- 3 tablespoons cider vinegar

- 2 tablespoons Worcestershire sauce

- 2 teaspoons liquid smoke

- 2 tablespoons molasses

- dash allspice

- 1/4 teaspoon freshly ground black pepper

- 1/8 to 1/4 teaspoon ground cayenne pepper

-

1 pound boneless chicken breasts

-

1 pound boneless chicken thighs

PREPARATION

1. In a medium saucepan over medium heat, melt the butter. When the butter is foamy, add the chopped onions and cook, stirring, until the onions are softened and lightly browned. Add the minced garlic and cook, stirring, for about 1 minute longer. Add the ketchup, apricot preserves, vinegar, Worcestershire sauce, liquid smoke, molasses, allspice, black pepper, and cayenne. Simmer for 5 minutes.
2. Put 1 1/2 cups of the sauce in the crockery insert of the slow cooker.
3. Reserve the remaining sauce; put in a container and refrigerate until serving time. Add the chicken pieces to the slow cooker. Cover and cook on LOW for 4 1/2 to 5 hours, or until the chicken is very tender and shreds easily. Using a fork, shred the chicken pieces.
4. Serve on split toasted buns with coleslaw and the extra extra barbecue sauce.
5. A menu might also include potato salad or baked potatoes, along with baked beans and sliced pickles and tomatoes. I like coleslaw and pickles on my barbecue, but other toppings might include jalapeno pepper rings, thinly sliced red onion, plain shredded cabbage, and sliced tomatoes or cucumbers.
6. Serves 8.

Smoked Sausage and Cabbage

INGREDIENTS

- 1 small head cabbage, coarsely shredded

- 1 large onion, coarsely chopped

- 1 1/2 to 2 pounds turkey Polish or smoked sausage kielbasa, cut in 1 to 2-inch pieces

- 1 cup apple juice

- 1 tablespoon dijon mustard

- 1 tablespoon cider vinegar

- 1 to 2 tablespoons brown sugar

- 1 teaspoon caraway seed, optional

- pepper, to taste

PREPARATION

1. Layer the cabbage, onion, and sausage in a 5- or 6-quart
    slow cooker (to make in a 3 1/2-quart cooker, use less
    cabbage or wilt it by boiling about 10 minutes, then drain
    and add). Whisk together the juice, mustard, vinegar, brown
    sugar, and caraway seed, if used; pour over slow cooker
    ingredients. Sprinkle with pepper, to taste. Cover and cook
    on low for 8 to 10 hours. Serve with potatoes and a tossed
    green salad, if desired.

Spanish Chicken With Rice

INGREDIENTS

- 4 chicken breast halves, skin removed

- 1/4 teaspoon salt

- 1/4 teaspoon pepper

- 1/4 teaspoon paprika

- 1 tablespoon vegetable oil

- 1 medium onion, chopped

- 1 small red pepper, chopped (or chopped roasted red pepper)

- 3 cloves garlic, minced

- 1/2 teaspoon dried rosemary

- 1 can (14 1/2 oz) crushed tomatoes

- 1 package (10 oz) frozen peas

PREPARATION

1. Season chicken with salt, pepper, paprika. In skillet, heat oil over medium heat and brown chicken on all sides. Transfer the chicken to slow cooker.
2. In a small bowl combine remaining ingredients, except frozen peas. Pour over chicken. Cover and cook on low 7 to 9 hours or on high 3 to 4 hours. One hour before serving, rinse peas in colander under warm water to thaw then add to crockpot. Serve this chicken dish over hot cooked rice.

Tami's Barbecued Chicken Legs

INGREDIENTS

-

6 to 8 frozen chicken legs•

-

1 bottle thick barbecue sauce

PREPARATION

1. Put frozen chicken legs in slow cooker. Pour BBQ sauce over them. Cover and cook on HIGH for 6 to 8 hours.
2. •Note: If starting with thawed chicken legs, you may remove skin or brown first to reduce fat, and cook on LOW for 6 to 8 hours.

Tami's Crockpot Chicken Mozzarella

INGREDIENTS

- 4 chicken leg quarters

- 2 tablespoons garlic pepper seasoning

- 1 can zucchini with tomato sauce

- 4 ounces shredded Mozzarella cheese

PREPARATION

1. Arrange the chicken in the slow cooker and sprinkle with seasoning. Pour zucchini with tomato sauce over chicken. Cover and cook on LOW for 6 to 8 hours. Sprinkle with cheese and cook until cheese melts, about 30 minutes.

White Chicken Chili

INGREDIENTS

- 4 boneless chicken breast halves, skin removed, cut in 1/2-inch pieces

- 1/2 cup chopped celery

- 1/2 cup chopped onion

- 2 cans (14.5 ounces each) stewed tomatoes, cut up

- 16 oz. med. salsa or picante sauce

- 1 can chick peas or Great Northern beans, drained

- 6 to 8 oz. sliced mushrooms

- Olive oil

PREPARATION

1. Brown chicken in 1 tablespoon olive oil. Chop celery, onion and mushrooms. Combine all ingredients in large slow cooker; stir and simmer on low heat for 6 to 8 hours. Serve with crusty bread or taco chips. •If you like it spicy, use hot salsa or picante sauce.

Slow Cooker Chicken and Black Beans

INGREDIENTS

- 3 to 4 boneless chicken breast halves, cut in strips

- 1 can (12 to 15 ounces) corn, drained

- 1 can (15 oz) black beans, rinsed and drained

- 2 teaspoons gound cumin

- 2 teaspoons chili powder

- 1 onion, halved and thinly sliced

- 1 green bell pepper, cut in strips

- 1 can (14.5 ounces) diced tomatoes

- 1 can (6 ounces) tomato paste

PREPARATION

1. Combine all ingredients in slow cooker. Cover and cook on low for 5 to 6 hours.
2. Garnish with shredded cheese, if desired. Serve fiesta chicken and black beans with warmed flour tortillas, or over rice.
3. Serves 4.

Chicken and Dressing, Slow Cooker

INGREDIENTS

-

1 bag seasoned stuffing mix, 14 to 16 ounces

-

3 to 4 cups cooked diced chicken

-

3 cans cream of chicken soup

-

1/2 cup milk

-

1 to 2 cups mild cheddar cheese, shredded

PREPARATION

1. Prepare stuffing mix according to package directions and place in 5 quart Crock Pot. Stir in 2 cans of Cream of Chicken soup. In a mixing bowl, stir together cubed chicken, 1 can cream of chicken soup and milk. Spread over stuffing in slow cooker. Sprinkle cheese over top. Cover and cook on Low for 4 to 6 hour or on High for 2 to 3 hours.
2. Serves 6 to 8.

Chicken and Mushrooms, Slow Cooker

INGREDIENTS

- 6 chicken breast halves, bone-in, skin removed

- 1 1/4 tsp. salt

- 1/4 tsp. pepper

- 1/4 tsp. paprika

- 2 teaspoons chicken bouillon granules

- 1 1/2 cup sliced mushrooms

- 1/2 cup sliced green onions

- 1/2 cup dry white wine

- 2/3 cup evaporated milk

- 5 tsp. cornstarch

- Minced fresh parsley

- hot cooked rice

PREPARATION

1. In a small bowl, mix salt, pepper and paprika. Rub all of the mixture into the chicken.
2. In a slow cooker, alternate layers of chicken, bouillon granules, mushrooms, and green onions. Pour wine over top. DO NOT STIR.
3. Cover and cook on HIGH for 2 1/2 to 3 hours or on LOW for 5 to 6 hours, or until chicken is tender but not falling off bone. Baste one about halfway through cooking if possible.
4. Remove chicken and vegetables to a platter with a slotted spoon.
5. Cover with foil and keep warm.
6. In a small saucepan, combine evaporated milk and cornstarch until smooth. Gradually stir in 2 cups of the cooking liquid. Stirring over medium heat, bring to a boil and boil for 1 to 2 minutes, or until thickened.
7. Spoon some of the sauce over chicken and garnish with minced parsley. Serve remaining sauce on the side.
8. Serve with hot cooked rice.

Chicken and Rice Parmesan, Slow Cooker

INGREDIENTS

- 1 envelope onion soup mix

- 1 can (10 3/4 ounces) condensed cream of mushroom soup,reduced fat

- 1 can (10 3/4 ounces) condensed cream of chicken soup,reduced fat

- 1 1/2 cups low or no fat milk

- 1 cup dry white wine

- 1 cup white rice

- 6 boneless chicken breast halves, without skin

- 2 tablespoons butter

- 2/3 cup grated Parmesan cheese

PREPARATION

1. Mix onion soup, condensed cream soups, milk, wine and rice. Spray Crock Pot w/pam. Lay chicken breasts in Crock Pot, top with 1 teaspoon of butter, pour soup mixture over all, then sprinkle with the Parmesan cheese. Cook on low 8 to 10 hours or on high for 4 to 6 hours. Serves 6.

Chicken and Shrimp

INGREDIENTS

- 2 pounds chicken, boneless thighs and breasts, skin removed, cut in chunks

- 2 tablespoons of extra virgin olive oil

- 1 cup chopped onion

- 2 cloves garlic, minced

- 1/4 cup parsley, minced

- 1/2 cup white wine

- 1 large can (15 ounces) tomato sauce

- 1 teaspoon dried leaf basil

- 1 pound uncooked shrimp, peeled and deveined

- salt and freshly ground black pepper, to taste

- 1 pound fettuccine, linguine, or spaghetti

PREPARATION

1. In a large skillet or sauté pan over medium heat, heat the olive oil. Add the chicken chunks and cook, stirring, until lightly browned. Remove chicken to slow cooker.
2. Add a little more oil to the pan and sauté the onion, garlic, and parsley for about 1 minute. Remove from heat and stir in the wine, tomato sauce, and dried basil. Pour the mixture over chicken in slow cooker.
3. Cover and cook on LOW for 4 to 5 hours.
4. Stir in shrimp, cover, and cook on LOW for about 1 hour longer.
5. Season with salt and freshly ground black pepper, to taste.
6. Just before the dish is done, cook the pasta in boiling salted water as directed on the package.

Chicken and Stuffing Recipe

INGREDIENTS

- 4 boneless chicken breast halves, without skin

- 4 slices Swiss cheese

- 1 can (10 1/2 ounce) condensed cream of chicken soup

- 1 can (10 1/2 ounce) condensed cream of mushroom soup

- 1 cup chicken broth

- 1/4 cup milk

- 2 to 3 cups Pepperidge Farm Herb Stuffing Mix or Homemade Stuffing Mix

- 1/2 cup melted butter •See Sandy's Notes

- salt and pepper to taste

PREPARATION

1.
Season chicken breasts with salt and pepper; place chicken breasts slow cooker.

2.
Pour chicken broth over chicken breasts.

3.

Put one slice of Swiss cheese on each breast.

4.

Combine both cans of soup and milk. Cover chicken breasts with soup mixture.

5.

Sprinkle stuffing mix over all. Drizzle melted butter on top.

6.

Cook on low for 6-8 hours.

Chicken Breasts in Creamy Creole Sauce

INGREDIENTS

- 1 bunch green onions (6 to 8, with most of the green part)

- 2 slices bacon

- 1 teaspoon Creole or Cajun seasoning

- 3 tablespoons butter

- 4 tablespoons flour

- 3/4 cup chicken broth

- 1 to 2 tablespoons tomato paste

- 4 boneless chicken breast halves

- 1/4 to 1/2 cup half and half or milk

PREPARATION

1. In a saucepan, melt butter over medium low heat. Add onions and bacon, cook and stir for 2 minutes. Add flour, stir and cook for 2 more minutes. Add chicken broth; cook until thick then add tomato paste. Place chicken breasts in the slow cooker/Crock Pot; add sauce mixture. Cover and cook on low for 6 to 7 hours, stirring after 3 hours. Stir in milk about 20 to 30 minutes before done. Serve over pasta or rice.
2. Serves 4.

Chicken Chili with Hominy

INGREDIENTS

- 2 pounds chicken breasts, boneless and skinless, cut in 1 to 1 1/2-inch pieces

- 1 medium onion, chopped

- 3 cloves garlic, thinly sliced

- 1 can (15 oz) white hominy, drained

- 1 can (14 oz) diced tomatoes, undrained

- 1 can (28 oz) tomatillos, drained and chopped

- 1 can (4 oz) mild green chiles

PREPARATION

1. Combine all ingredients in slow cooker; stir to blend all ingredients. Cover and cook on low for 7 to 9 hours, or high for 4 to 4 1/2 hours.
2. Serves 4 to 6.

Chicken Delish

INGREDIENTS

- 6 to 8 boneless, skinless chicken breast halves

- lemon juice

- salt and pepper, to taste

- celery salt or seasoned salt, to taste

- paprika, to taste

- 1 can cream of celery soup

- 1 can cream of mushroom soup

- 1/3 cup dry white wine

- grated Parmesan cheese, to taste

- cooked rice

PREPARATION

1. Rinse chicken; pat dry. Season with lemon juice, salt, pepper, celery salt, and paprika. Place chicken in slow cooker. In medium bowl mix soups with wine. Pour over chicken breasts. Sprinkle with Parmesan cheese. Cover and cook on low for 6 to 8 hours. Serve chicken with sauce over hot cooked rice, and pass the Parmesan cheese.
2. Serves 4 to 6.

Chicken Enchiladas for the Slow Cooker

INGREDIENTS

-

1 pkg. chicken breasts (1 - 1 1/2 lbs)

-

1 jar chicken gravy

-

1 4 oz can green chiles, chopped

-

1 onion, chopped

-

corn tortillas

-

shredded cheese

PREPARATION

1. Combine chicken, gravy, green chiles, and chopped onion in slow cooker; cover and cook on LOW for 5 to 6 hours. Take chicken out of sauce and shred. Fill corn tortillas with chicken and sauce. Top with shredded cheese and roll. Place in baking dish. Pour excess sauce over and sprinkle with more shredded cheese. Bake at 350° for approximately 15 to 20 minutes.
2. Serves 4 to 6.

Chicken Las Vegas

INGREDIENTS

- 6 boneless chicken breast halves, without skin

- 1 can cream of mushroom soup

- 1/2 pint. sour cream

- 1 (6 oz.) jar dried, chipped beef

PREPARATION

1. Mix together soup, sour cream and dried beef. Roll chicken in the mixture, coating well; place in crockpot. Pour remaining mixture over chicken. Cover and cook on LOW for 5 to 7 hours, until chicken is tender but not dried out. Serve with hot cooked rice or noodles.
2. Serves 6.

Chicken Parisienne for the Slow Cooker

INGREDIENTS

- 6 to 8 chicken breast halves

- salt, pepper, and paprika

- 1/2 cup dry white wine

- 1 (10 1/2 oz.) can cream of mushroom soup

- 8 ounces sliced mushrooms

- 1 cup sour cream

- 1/4 cup flour

PREPARATION

1. Sprinkle chicken breasts with salt, pepper and paprika. Place in slow cooker. Mix wine, soup and mushrooms until well combined. Pour over chicken. Sprinkle with paprika. Cover and cook on low for 6 to 8 hours, or until chicken is tender but not too dry. Mix sour cream and flour together; add to the Crock Pot. Cook for about 20 minutes longer, until heated through.
2. Serve with rice or noodles.
3. Serves 6 to 8.

Chicken Reuben Casserole, Slow Cooker

INGREDIENTS

- 32 ounces sauerkraut (jar or bag), rinsed and drained

- 1 cup Russian dressing

- 4 to 6 boneless chicken breast halves, skin removed

- 1 tablespoon prepared mustard

- 1 cup shredded Swiss cheese or Monterey Jack

PREPARATION

1. Layer half of the sauerkraut in the bottom of the pot. Pour 1/3 cup dressing over it; place 2 to 3 chicken breasts on top and spread the mustard on chicken. Top with the remaining sauerkraut and chicken breasts; pour another 1/3 cup of dressing over all and reserve the remaining 1/3 cup of dressing for serving.
2. Cover and cook on low for about 4 hours, or until chicken is cooked through and tender. Sprinkle Swiss cheese and cook until cheese is melted.
3. Serve with reserved dressing.
4. Serves 4 to 6.

Chicken with Cranberries

INGREDIENTS

- 6 boneless, skinless chicken breasts

- 1 small onion, chopped

- 1 cup fresh cranberries

- 1 teaspoon salt

- 1/4 teaspoon ground cinnamon

- 1/4 teaspoon ground ginger

- 3 tablespoons brown sugar or honey

- 1 cup orange juice

- 3 tablespoons flour mixed with 2 tablespoons cold water

PREPARATION

1. Place all ingredients, except flour and water mixture, in the slow cooker or Crock Pot. Cover and cook on low 6 to 7 hours, until chicken is tender. Add flour mixture in the last 15 to 20 minutes and cook until thickened. Taste and adjust seasonings.
2. Serves 4.

Chicken with Dressing and Gravy, Slow Cooker

INGREDIENTS

- 1 package (6 ounces) seasoned stuffing crumbs (a "stove top" type stuffing mix)

- 1 large potato, cut in small dice

- 1 bunch green onions, chopped

- 2 ribs celery, chopped

- 1/2 cup water

- 3 tablespoons butter, divided

- 1 teaspoon poultry seasoning, divided

- 1 to 1 1/2 pounds chicken tenderloins or boneless breasts

- 1 jar (12 ounces) chicken gravy, such as Heinz Homestyle Chicken Gravy

PREPARATION

1. In a lightly buttered or sprayed crockpot, toss stuffing crumbs with diced potato, green onion, celery, 2 tablespoons melted butter and 1/2 cup water. Sprinkle with about 1/2 teaspoon of poultry seasoning. Top stuffing with chicken pieces; drizzle with remaining butter and poultry seasoning. Pour gravy over chicken. Cover and cook on low for 6 to 7 hours.

Chicken with Macaroni and Smoked Gouda Cheese

INGREDIENTS

-

1 1/2 pounds chicken tenders, boneless

-

2 small zucchini, halved and sliced 1/8-inch thick

-

1 package chicken gravy mix (approx. 1 oz)

-

2 tablespoons water

-

salt and pepper to taste

-

pinch of ground nutmeg, fresh if possible

-

8 ounces smoked Gouda cheese, grated

-

2 tablespoons evaporated milk or light cream

-

1 large tomato, chopped

-

4 cups cooked macaroni or small shell pasta

PREPARATION

1. Cut chicken into 1-inch cubes; place in crockpot. Add zucchini, gravy mix, water, and seasoning. Cover and cook for 5 to 6 hours on low. Add smoked gouda cheese, milk or cream, and chopped tomato to the crockpot during the last 20 minutes, or while the macaroni is cooking. Stir in hot cooked macaroni.
2. Chicken recipe serves 4.

Chicken With Pearl Onions and Mushrooms, Slow Cooker

INGREDIENTS

- 4 to 6 boneless chicken breast halves, cut in 1-inch chunks

- 1 can (10 3/4 ounces) cream of chicken or cream of chicken and mushroom soup

- 8 ounces sliced mushrooms

- 1 bag (16 ounces) frozen pearl onions

- salt and pepper, to taste

- parsley, chopped, for garnish

PREPARATION

1. Wash chicken and pat dry. Cut into chunks about 1/2 to 1-inch and put in a large bowl. Add the soup, mushrooms, and onions; stir to combine. Spray the slow cooker insert with cooking spray.
2. Spoon the chicken mixture into the crockpot and sprinkle with salt and pepper.
3. Cover and cook on LOW for 6 to 8 hours, stirring about halfway through the cooking time, if possible.
4. Garnish with fresh chopped parsley, if desired, and serve over hot cooked rice or with potatoes.
5. Serves 4 to 6.

Chicken With Pineapple

INGREDIENTS

- 1 to 1 1/2 pounds chicken tenders, cut in 1-inch pieces

- 2/3 cup pineapple preserves

- 1 tablespoon plus 1 teaspoon teriyaki sauce

- 2 cloves garlic sliced thinly

- 1 tablespoon dried minced onion (or 1 bunch fresh green onions, chopped)

- 1 tablespoon lemon juice

- 1/2 teaspoon ground ginger

- dash cayenne, to taste

- 1 package (10 oz) sugar snap peas, thawed

PREPARATION

1. Place chicken pieces in slow cooker/Crock Pot.
2. Combine preserves, teriyaki sauce, garlic, onion, lemon juice, ginger, and cayenne; stir well. Spoon over chicken, toss to coat.
3. Cover and cook on low 6 to 7 hours. Add peas last 30 minutes.
4. Serves 4.

Country Captain Chicken

INGREDIENTS

- 2 medium-size Granny Smith apples, cored and diced (unpeeled)

- 1/4 cup finely chopped onion

- 1 small green bell pepper, seeded and finely chopped

- 3 cloves garlic, minced

- 2 tablespoons raisins or currants

- 2 to 3 teaspoons curry powder

- 1 teaspoon ground ginger

- 1/4 teaspoon ground red pepper, or to taste

- 1 can (about 14 1/2 oz.) diced tomatoes

- 6 boneless chicken breast halves, skin removed

- 1/2 cup chicken broth

- 1 cup long-grain converted white rice

- 1 pound medium to large shrimp, shelled and deveined, uncooked, optional

- 1/3 cup slivered almonds

- kosher salt

- Chopped parsley

PREPARATION

1. In a 4- to 6-quart slow cooker, combine diced apples, onion, bell pepper, garlic, golden raisins or currants, curry powder, ginger, and ground red pepper; stir in tomatoes.
2. Arrange the chicken over the tomato mixture, overlapping pieces slightly. Pour chicken broth over the chicken breast halves. Cover and cook on LOW until chicken is very tender when pierced with a fork, about 4 to 6 hours.
3. Remove chicken to a warm plate, cover lightly, and keep warm in a 200° F oven or warming drawer.
4. Stir the rice into cooking liquid. Increase temperature to high; cover and cook, stirring once or twice, until rice is almost tender, about 35 minutes. Stir in shrimp, if using; cover and cook for about 15 minutes longer, until shrimp are opaque in center; cut to test.
5. Meanwhile, toast almonds in a small nonstick frying pan over medium heat until golden brown, stirring occasionally. Set aside.
6. To serve the dish, season rice mixture to taste with salt. Mound in a warm serving dish; arrange chicken on top. Sprinkle with parsley and almonds.

Country Chicken and Mushrooms

INGREDIENTS

- 1 jar country gravy

- 4 to 6 chicken breasts

- 8 ounces sliced mushrooms

- salt and pepper to taste

PREPARATION

1. Combine all ingredients; cover and cook on low for 6 to 7 hours. Serve with rice or noodles.
2. Serves 4 to 6.

Cranberry Chicken
INGREDIENTS

- 2 pounds boneless chicken breasts, skin removed

- 1/2 cup chopped onion

- 2 teaspoons vegetable oil

- 2 teaspoons salt

- 1/2 teaspoon ground cinnamon

- 1/4 teaspoon ground ginger

- 1/8 teaspoon ground nutmeg

- dash ground allspice

- 1 cup orange juice

- 2 teaspoons finely grated orange peel

- 2 cups fresh or frozen cranberries

- 1/4 cup brown sugar

PREPARATION

1. Brown chicken pieces and onion in oil; sprinkle with salt.
2. Add browned chicken, onions and other ingredients to crock pot.
3. Cover and cook on LOW 5 1/2 to 7 hours.
4. If desired, thicken juices near the end of cooking time with a mixture of about 2 tablespoons cornstarch combined with 2 tablespoons cold water.

Creamy Italian Chicken

INGREDIENTS

- 4 boneless skinless chicken breast halves

- 1 envelope Italian salad dressing mix

- 1/3 cup water

- 1 package (8 ozs.) cream cheese, softened

- 1 can (10 3/4 ozs.) condensed cream of chicken soup, undiluted

- 1 can (4 ozs.) mushroom stems and pieces, drained

- Hot cooked rice or noodles

PREPARATION

1. Place the chicken breast halves in a slow cooker. Combine salad dressing mix and water; pour over chicken. Cover and cook on LOW for 3 hours. In a small mixing bowl, whisk together cream cheese and soup until blended. Stir in mushrooms. Pour cream cheese mixture over chicken. Cook 1 to 3 hours longer or until chicken juices run clear. Serve Italian chicken with rice or hot cooked noodles.
2. Serves 4.

Crock Caramel Nut Rolls

INGREDIENTS

- 2 tubes (7 to 8 ounces each) refrigerated biscuits•

- 3/4 cup packed brown sugar

- 1 teaspoon ground cinnamon

- 1/4 cup finely chopped pecans or walnuts

- 6 tablespoons melted butter

PREPARATION

1. Generously butter a 3 to 4-quart slow cooker insert or a casserole or baking dish which will fit in a larger slow cooker.
2. Mix brown sugar, cinnamon, and chopped nuts together.
3. Dip each refrigerator biscuit in melted butter to coat, then in the brown sugar, cinnamon, and nut mixture.
4. Layer in the prepared slow cooker insert or baking dish.
5. Sprinkle any remaining brown sugar mixture over the top.
6. Cook on high for 1 1/2 to 2 hours, until the biscuits are baked.

7.   I took mine out after about 1 hour and 45 minutes. They were done, but slow cooker temperatures can vary.
8.   I used 8 of my frozen make-ahead biscuits, thawed and cut in half horizontally, layered in a 3-quart cooker (pictured). A baking dish in a larger oval or round cooker would make it easier to get the biscuits out in one piece.
9.   You could also use small homemade biscuits or about 1 pound of thawed bread dough, cut in 16 to 20 pieces.

Crockpot Apple Butter

INGREDIENTS

-

apples, peeled, cored and cut in quarters, to fill a 4-quart crockpot to 1 1/2 to 2 inches from top

-

4 tsp. cinnamon

-

1/2 tsp cloves

-

1/2 tsp salt

-

3 cups sugar

-

4 tablespoons water

PREPARATION

1. Combine all ingredients in slow cooker. Cover and cook on HIGH until hot, then turn to LOW and cook all day (7 to 10 hours). When it is done and apples are fully cooked down put small amounts into food processor and pulse until smooth.
2. NOTE: If you are canning this, put into clean, sterilized jars and seal while hot, then process half-pints or pints 5 minutes in boiling water canner. 1,001 feet to 6,000 feet, process for 10 minutes, and above 6,000 feet, 15 minutes.

Crockpot Apple Butter II

INGREDIENTS

-

7 cups applesauce, natural

-

2 cups apple cider

-

1 1/2 cups honey

-

1 tsp ground cinnamon

-

1/4 tsp ground cloves, optional

-

1/2 tsp allspice

PREPARATION

1. In a slow cooker, combine all ingredients. Cover and cook on LOW for 14 to 15 hours or until mixture is a deep brown.
2. Spoon hot apple butter into hot sterilized jars and seal, then process half-pints or pints 10 minutes in a boiling water bath.
3. Makes 4 pints or 8 half-pint jars.

Crockpot Apple Crisp Dessert

INGREDIENTS

- 6 medium cooking apples, peeled, cored, sliced

- 1 1/2 cups flour

- 1 cup packed brown sugar

- 1 tablespoon cinnamon

- 1/2 teaspoon nutmeg

- 1/4 teaspoon ginger

- 3/4 cup butter, softened

Topping Suggestions:

- Vanilla ice cream

- Maraschino cherries

- Whipped cream or whipped topping

PREPARATION

1. Generously butter the crock pot (slow cooker). Arrange apple slices in bottom of the pot. In a bowl, combine flour, sugar, spices and butter with fingers or a fork until crumbly.
2. Cover the apples with the crumble mixture. Tamp down lightly.
3. Cook on HIGH for 3 to 4 hours, or until apples are tender.
4. Serve in dessert dishes with any or all of the suggested toppings.
5. Enjoy...good on a cool, crisp Fall day!

Crockpot Bread Pudding

INGREDIENTS

- 5 eggs, beaten

- 3 1/2 cups milk

- 2 teaspoons vanilla

- 2 Tablespoons (yes!) ground cinnamon

- 1/2 teaspoon salt

- 6 cups plain breadcrumbs (or more to make mixture as thick as cooked oatmeal when mixed with all ingredients)

- 3/4 cup packed brown sugar

- 1 Tablespoon butter or margarine, melted

- 1/2 cup raisins (optional)

- One mashed or sliced banana (optional)

PREPARATION

1. Mix all ingredients together until breadcrumbs are thoroughly wet, and mixture is smooth like thick oatmeal. Place mixture in a generously greased slow cooker. Cook on high for 4 to 5 hours,or until a knife inserted in center comes out fairly clean.
2. NOTE: For the last 1/2 hour of cooking, lift the lid a "crack" by putting a spoon or fork between it and the pot, to let the excess moisture escape; otherwise you will have a clear liquid all around the bread pudding.

Crockpot Bread Pudding II

INGREDIENTS

- 5 eggs, beaten

- 3 1/2 cups milk

- 2 teaspoons vanilla

- 2 Tablespoons (yes!) ground cinnamon

- 1/2 teaspoon salt

- 6 cups plain bread crumbs (or more to make mixture as thick as cooked oatmeal when mixed with all ingredients)

- 3/4 cup packed brown sugar

- 1 Tablespoon butter or margarine, melted

- 1/2 cup raisins (optional)

- One mashed or sliced banana (optional)

PREPARATION

1. Mix all ingredients together until bread crumbs are thoroughly wet, and mixture is smooth like thick oatmeal. Place mixture in a generously greased slow cooker. Cook on high for 4 to 5 hours,or until a knife inserted in center comes out fairly clean.
2. NOTE: For the last 1/2 hour of cooking, lift the lid a "crack" by putting a spoon or fork between it and the pot, to let the excess moisture escape; otherwise you will have a clear liquid all around the bread pudding.

Crockpot Candy

INGREDIENTS

-
2 lbs. white almond bark

-
4 ounces dipping chocolate, milk chocolate or chocolate almond bark

-
12 oz. pkg. semisweet chocolate chips

-
2 1/2 cups dry roasted peanuts

-
1 cup raisins

PREPARATION

1. Combine almond bark, milk chocolate, chocolate chips, and peanuts in crockpot. Turn to LOW and stir every 15 minutes for 45 minutes. Stir in raisins and cook 15 minutes longer.
2. Drop on waxed paper and let cool. When firm, store in an air-tight container.

Crock Pot Cranberries

INGREDIENTS

-

1 pound fresh cranberries

-

2 cups granulated sugar

-

1/4 cup water

PREPARATION

1. Combine cranberries with sugar and water in Crock Pot. Cover and cook on high 2 to 3 hours until cranberries begin to pop. Serve with turkey, pork, or chicken.

Crockpot Orange Cinnamon Bread Pudding

INGREDIENTS

- 6 slices bread, about 6 ounces, torn into small pieces

- 1/2 cup golden or dark raisins

- 1 can (12 ounces) evaporated milk

- 4 large eggs

- 2 tablespoons melted butter

- 6 ounces orange juice concentrate

- 4 large eggs

- 1 cup sugar

- 1/2 teaspoon ground cinnamon

- 1 tablespoon vanilla extract

PREPARATION

1. Generously butter a 1 1/2-quart souffle dish or 7-cup Pyrex glass straight-sided container/casserole.
2. Put bread and raisins in a large bowl. Set aside.
3. In another bowl, whisk milk and eggs with melted butter, orange juice concentrate, sugar, cinnamon, and vanilla; pour over the bread mixture and blend well.
4. Pour into prepared bowl/casserole.
5. Tear off a 16-inch length of foil and fold lengthwise twice to form a sturdy lift for the finished pudding.
6. Fit the foil in the slow cooker, letting the ends lay outside. Pour about 1 cup of very hot water into the crockpot. Place the bread pudding in the crockery, arrange foil "handles" to the inside and cover the pot.
7. Cook on HIGH for 2 1/2 hours. Using pot holders, gently use the "handles" to lift the dish up out of the pot so that you can get a grip on the outside of the dish. Place on a rack to cool slightly.
8. Serve warm with vanilla sauce or an orange sauce.

Crock Pot Peach Butter

INGREDIENTS

- 6 cups unsweetened peaches

- 3 cups white sugar

- 1 1/2 cups apricot nectar

- 2 tablespoons orange or lemon juice

- 1 teaspoon vanilla

PREPARATION

1. Put peaches through food mill or food processor.
2. Combine all ingredients in a slow cooker.
3. Cover and cook on LOW for 3 hours, stirring occasionally.
4. Uncover and continue cooking until excess liquid cooks away, about 5 to 8 hours.
5. Transfer to containers. Seal and refrigerate or freeze for longer storage.

Crockpot Pound Cake

INGREDIENTS

-

1 box (16 ounces pound cake mix

-

1/4 cup light brown sugar, firmly packed

-

1 tablespoon all-purpose flour

-

1/4 cup finely chopped pecans

-

1 teaspoon ground cinnamon

-

1 teaspoon melted butter

-

.

-

Vanilla Glaze:

-

1/2 cup confectioners' sugar

-

1/4 teaspoon vanilla

-

2 to 3 tablespoons milk

PREPARATION

1. Mix cake mix according to package directions. Pour batter into well greased and floured 2 pound coffee tin (make sure it will fit in your crockpot with cover) or baking dish which holds batter and fits in your crockpot. Combine sugar, flour, nuts, cinnamon, and butter; sprinkle over cake batter. Place can in slow cooker. Cover top of can with 8 layers of paper towels. Cover slow cooker and bake on high for 3 to 4 hours.

2. Cool on rack for 5 minutes; unmold. Combine vanilla glaze ingredients until smooth; drizzle over cake.

Crockpot Pumpkin Bread

INGREDIENTS

- 1 cup all-purpose flour

- 1 1/2 tsp baking powder

- 1 tsp pumpkin pie spice

- 1/2 cup brown sugar, firmly packed

- 2 Tb vegetable oil

- 2 eggs, slightly beaten

- 1/2 cup pumpkin puree (canned)

- 1/4 cup raisins, finely chopped

PREPARATION

1. Combine flour, baking powder and pumpkin pie spice in a bowl; set aside.
2. In mixing bowl, combine brown sugar and vegetable oil; beat until well blended. Beat in eggs. Add pumpkin and mix well. Stir in flour mixture and beat with a wooden spoon just until combined. Stir in raisins.
3. Pour pumpkin mixture into 2 well-greased and floured half pint canning jars with straight sides. Cover jars tightly with greased aluminum foil.
4. Place a rack or piece of somewhat crumpled foil in 3-1/2 or 4 qt. crockpot. Place jars on rack or foil.
5. Cover and cook on HIGH setting for about 1 1/2 hours or until a wooden pick or cake tester inserted in center comes out clean.
6. Remove jars and place on wire rack; cool 10 minutes. Carefully remove bread from jars. Cool completely on wire rack. Makes 2 loaves.

Crock Pot Rice Pudding

INGREDIENTS

- 2 1/2 cups cooked rice

- 1 1/2 cups scalded milk

- 2/3 cup white or brown sugar

- 3 eggs, beaten

- 1 tsp. salt

- 2 tbsp. vanilla

- 1 tsp. cinnamon

- 1 tsp. nutmeg

- 1/2 cup raisins

- 3 tablespoons soft butter

PREPARATION

1. Combine all ingredients. Pour into a buttered baking dish which will fit into slow cooker. (This can also be poured directly into a buttered crockpot.) Cook on high 1 1/2 to 2 hours. Stir every 10 minutes during first 30 minutes. Recipe can be doubled.

Crock Pot Rice Pudding with Fruit

INGREDIENTS

- 1 package (6 ounces) dried cranberries

- 1 package (4 ounces) dried blueberries

- 1 can (12 ounces) evaporated milk

- 1 1/2 cups water

- 8 ounces frozen orange juice concentrate

- 3/4 cup sugar

- 1 cup heavy cream

- Dash salt

- 1/4 teaspoon ground cinnamon

- 1 cup short-grain Arborio rice

PREPARATION

1. Spray the inside of the crockery insert with nonstick cooking spray.
2. Combine all ingredients and pour into the slow cooker.
3. Cover and cook on LOW for 4 to 5 hours or on HIGH for 2 to 2 1/2 hours, or until rice is tender and mixture has thickened.
4. Stir the mixture about halfway through the cooking time and shortly before it's done.
5. 6 Servings

Crockpot Fried Apples

INGREDIENTS

- 3 pounds Granny Smith apples, peeled, cored, and sliced

- 1 teaspoon cinnamon

- dash of fresh grated nutmeg, optional

- 3 tablespoons cornstarch

- 1 cup granulated sugar

- 1 to 2 tablespoons of butter, cut in small pieces

PREPARATION

1. Place apple slices in the slow cooker/Crock Pot; stir in remaining ingredients and dot with the butter. Cover and cook on low for about 6 hours, or until apples are tender but not mushy. Stir about halfway through cooking.
2. Makes 2 1/2 to 3 cups.

Curried Fruit Bake

INGREDIENTS

- 1 package prunes, (16 oz) pitted

- 1 package dried apricots (11 oz)

- 1 can pineapple chunks (20 ounces) drained

- 1 can peaches; sliced (1 lb 13 oz)

- 1 cup brown sugar

- 1/2 teaspoon curry powder

- 12 ounces ginger ale

PREPARATION

1. Combine all ingredients in slow cooker. Cover and cook on LOW for 4 to 5 hours or HIGH for about 1 1/2 to 2 hours.

Easy Cherry Cobbler

INGREDIENTS

- 1 16 oz can cherry pie filling, light

- 1 pkg cake mix for 1 layer cake, or sweet muffin mix

- 1 egg

- 3 tablespoons evaporated milk

- 1/2 teaspoon cinnamon

- 1/2 cup chopped nuts, optional

PREPARATION

1. Put pie filling in lightly buttered 3 1/2-quart Crock Pot and cook on high for 30 minutes. Mix together the remaining ingredients and spoon onto the hot pie filling. Cover and cook for 2 to 3 hours on low. You may also use a lightly greased souffle dish in a larger slow cooker.
2. 6 servings.

Easy Chocolate Clusters

INGREDIENTS

- 2 pounds white candy coating, or almond bark, broken into small pieces

- 2 cups (12 ounces) semisweet chocolate chips

- 4 ounces German's Sweet Chocolate

- 24 ounces dry roasted peanuts

PREPARATION

1. In crockpot, combine the white candy coating or almond bark, German's Sweet Chocolate, and semisweet chocolate chips. Cover and cook on HIGH for 1 hour; reduce to LOW. Cover and cook 1 hour longer, or until candy is melted, stirring every 12 to 15 minutes. Stir in roasted peanuts, mixing well. Drop peanut clusters by teaspoonfuls onto waxed paper; let stand until set. Store candy at room temperature.
2. Makes about 3 to 4 dozen chocolate peanut clusters.

Easy Slow Cooker Applesauce

INGREDIENTS

- 8 to 10 apples, peeled, cored, and cut in chunks

- 1/3 cup apple juice or water

- 1 scant teaspoon cinnamon

- 1/2 cup packed brown sugar

PREPARATION

1. Combine all ingredients in a slow cooker.
2. Cover and cook on LOW for 7 to 9 hours.
3. Stir to blend and mash lightly, if desired.
4. Serves 8.

Favorite Baked Custard

INGREDIENTS

- 2 cups milk, scalded

- 3 eggs, slightly beaten

- 1/3 cup granulated sugar

- 1 teaspoon vanilla

- 1/8 teaspoon salt

- nutmeg

- coconut, optional

PREPARATION

1. Scald milk and let cool slightly. Combine eggs, sugar, vanilla, and salt. Slowly stir in the milk. Pour into a buttered 1-qt baking dish which fits in your slow cooker. Sprinkle with nutmeg and coconut, if desired. Cover baking dish with foil.
2. Set baking dish on a trivet or ring of foil in slow cooker.
3. Pour hot water around baking dish to about 1 inch deep. Cover pot and cook on HIGH for 2 to 2 1/2 hours, or until knife inserted in custard comes out clean.
4. Serve warm or chilled.
5. Makes 6 servings.

Flowerpot Banana Bread
INGREDIENTS

- 2 cups flour

- 1 teaspoon baking soda

- 1/2 teaspoon salt

- 1/2 cup butter

- 1 cup sugar

- 2 eggs

- 1 cup ripe bananas; mashed, 2 to 3 medium bananas

- 1/3 cup milk

- 1 teaspoon lemon juice

- 1/2 cup walnuts, chopped

- 1 flower pot, terra cotta, about 6 1/2 inch size, to fit in crockpot

PREPARATION

1. Wash a new flower pot well; grease then line with waxed paper, cutting to fit. Note: Make sure the flower pot fits in your crockpot, or use a 2-pound coffee can. Grease the waxed paper.
2. Mix flour, baking soda and salt. In a separate bowl, cream butter, then add sugar, eggs and bananas, blending thoroughly. Combine milk and lemon juice to banana mixture, alternately add flour and milk mixture, then stir in nuts.
3. Pour mixture into prepared flower pot and place in crockpot. Place liner in base. Cover with 2 to 3 paper towels. Cover crockpot and cook on low 5 to 6 hours. Do not lift lid to check on it until last hour.

Fresh Apple Coffeecake
INGREDIENTS

-

2 cups biscuit baking mix

-

2/3 cup applesauce

-

1/4 cup milk

-

2 tablespoons granulated sugar

-

2 tablespoons butter, softened or melted

-

2 apples, peeled, cored and diced

-

1 teaspoon cinnamon

-

1 teaspoon vanilla

-

1 egg, lightly beaten

-

Streusel

-

1/4 cup biscuit mix

-

1/4 cup brown sugar

- 2 tablespoons firm butter

- 1 teaspoon cinnamon

- 1/4 cup chopped nuts, if desired

PREPARATION

1. Combine first 9 ingredients. Mix until well blended.
2. Spread in a lightly greased 3 1/2 quart Crock Pot (or spread in a lightly greased baking dish which fits in a larger sized Crock Pot).
3. Combine streusel ingredients with a fork or pastry blender; sprinkle over the batter.
4. Cover and cook on high for about 2 1/2 hours, until a toothpick inserted in the center comes out clean. Uncover and let the cake cool in the pot.
5. When cool enough to handle, loosen it from the sides and lift out carefully with a flexible spatula, or loosen sides and invert the pot slightly and remove with your hand (you could hold a small piece of foil or waxed paper).

Ginger Brown Bread

INGREDIENTS

- 1 gingerbread mix (approximately 14 to 15 ounces)

- 1/4 cup yellow cornmeal

- 1 tsp. salt

- 1 1/2 cups milk

- 1/2 cup raisins

PREPARATION

1. Combine gingerbread mix with cornmeal and salt in mixing bowl; stir in milk, mixing just until batter is moistened.
2. Beat with electric mixer at medium speed for 2 minutes; stir in raisins.
3. Pour into a greased and floured 7-cup mold. Cover with foil and tie.
4. Put a trivet or rack in slow cooker. I use slightly crumpled foil as a rack. Pour 1 1/2 cups hot water in the pot. Place the filled mold on the rack or foil in the crockpot.
5. Cover and cook on HIGH for 3 to 4 hours or until the bread is done.
6. Remove from crockpot and cool on a wire rack for 5 minutes.
7. Loosen edges carefully with a knife and turn out on a rack to cool slightly.
8. Serve warm with butter or cream cheese spread.

Home-Style Bread Pudding

INGREDIENTS

- 2 eggs, slightly beaten

- 2 1/4 cups whole milk

- 1 teaspoon vanilla

- 1/2 to 1 teaspoon cinnamon

- 1/4 teaspoon salt

- 2 cups 1-inch bread cubes

- 1/2 cup brown sugar

- 1/2 cup raisins or chopped dates

PREPARATION

1. In medium mixing bowl, combine eggs with milk, vanilla, cinnamon, salt, bread, sugar, and raisins or dates. Pour into 1 1/2-quart baking or souffle dish which fits in your slow cooker. Place metal trivet (or aluminum foil shaped in a ring to keep the dish off the bottom of the pot) or rack in bottom of crockpot. Add 1/2 cup hot water to the crockpot. Set the baking dish on trivet or foil ring. Cover and cook on high for about 2 hours, until set.
2. Serve bread pudding warm or cool, with sauce of your choice or plain.
3. Makes 4 to 6 servings.

Hot Caramel Apples

INGREDIENTS

- 4 large tart apples, cored

- 1/2 cup apple juice

- 1/2 cup brown sugar, packed

- 12 red-hot cinnamon candies

- 4 tablespoons butter

- 8 caramels

- 1/4 teaspoon ground cinnamon

PREPARATION

1. Peel about 3/4-inch off the top of each apple; place in crockpot. Pour apple juice over apples. Fill the center of each apple with 2 tablespoons of brown sugar, 3 cinnamon candies, 1 tablespoon of butter, and 2 caramels. Sprinkle with a little cinnamon. Cover and cook on low for 4 to 6 hours or until apples are tender. Serve warm as is or with cream or whipped topping.
2. Makes 4 baked apples.

Hot Fruit Compote

INGREDIENTS

- 1 can peaches, drained

- 1 can pears, drained

- 1 can pineapple chunks, drained

- 1 cup brown sugar

- 1 tsp. cinnamon

- 1/2 stick butter or margarine (4oz)

- 1 can cherry pie filling

PREPARATION

1. Cut all fruit into bite-size pieces. Add rest of ingredients. Stir all together. Cover and cook on low 3 to 6 hours. Use as a side dish for breakfast or a meal, or as a topping for a dessert.

Hot Fruit Dessert

INGREDIENTS

- 3 grapefruit, peeled and sectioned

- 1 can (11 oz) mandarin orange sections, drained

- 1 can (16 oz) fruit cocktail, well drained

- 1 can (20 oz) pineapple chunks, well drained

- 1 can (16 oz) sliced peaches, well drained

- 3 bananas, sliced, optional

- 1 tablespoon lemon juice

- 1 can (21 oz) cherry pie filling

PREPARATION

1. Combine all ingredients in slow cooker and toss gently to blend. Cover and cook on low for 3 to 5 hours.
2. Makes about 2 quarts of fruit. Serve with whipped cream or whipped topping.

Hot Spiced Fruit

INGREDIENTS

- 1 large can (28 to 29 ounces) peach slices, drained (28 to 29 ounces)

- 1 can pineapple tidbits with natural juices, undrained (8 to 16 ounces)

- 1 large can (28 to 29 ounces) pear slices, drained (28 to 29 ounces)

- 1 can (15 ounces) mixed chunky fruit

- maraschino cherries, drained, about 1/2 cup, or as desired

- 1 tablespoon cornstarch

- 1 1/2 teaspoons ground cinnamon

- 1 teaspoon ground nutmeg

- 1/2 cup brown sugar

- 4 tablespoons butter

PREPARATION

1. Combine all ingredients in the slow cooker; stir gently.
2. Cover and cook on LOW for about 4 to 6 hours or on HIGH for 2 to 3 hours. Serve with heavy cream or a dollop of sour cream, if desired.
3. Serves 8.

Indian Pudding

INGREDIENTS

- 3 cups milk

- 1/2 cup cornmeal

- 1/2 teaspoon salt

- 3 eggs

- 1/4 cup light brown sugar

- 1/3 cup molasses

- 2 tablespoons butter

- 1/2 teaspoon ground cinnamon

- 1/4 teaspoon ground allspice

- 1/2 teaspoon ground ginger

- 2/3 cup chopped dates or chopped raisins

PREPARATION

1. Lightly grease crockpot. Preheat on high for 20 minutes. Meanwhile bring milk, cornmeal and salt to a boil. Boil, stirring constantly, for 5 minutes. Cover and simmer an additional 10 minutes. In a large bowl, combine eggs, brown sugar, molasses, butter, and spices. Gradually beat in hot cornmeal mixture; whisk until smooth. Stir in raisins or finely chopped dates. Pour into crock and cook on high for 2 to 3 hours or low for 6 to 8 hours.

Lemon-Poppyseed Upside Down Cake

INGREDIENTS

- 1 pkg. Lemon-Poppyseed Bread Mix

- 1 egg

- 8 ounces light sour cream

- 1/2 cup water

-

.

- Sauce:

- 1 tablespoon butter

- 3/4 cup water

- 1/2 cup sugar

- juice from one lemon (about 1/4 cup)

PREPARATION

1. Mix the first 4 ingredients together until well moistened. Spread batter in a lightly greased 3 1/2 quart slow cooker/Crock Pot. Combine sauce ingredients in a small saucepan; bring to a boil. Pour boiling mixture over the batter; cover and cook on high for 2 to 2 1/2 hours. Edges will be slightly browned. Turn heat off and leave in the pot for about 30 minutes with cover slightly ajar. When cool enough to handle, hold a large plate over the top of the pot then invert.

Luscious Lemon Cheesecake

INGREDIENTS

-

Crust:

-

1 cup vanilla wafer crumbs

-

1/2 teaspoon lemon zest

-

1 tablespoons sugar

-

3 tablespoons butter, melted

Filling:

-

16 ounces cream cheese, softened

-

2/3 cup granulated sugar

-

2 large eggs

-

1 tablespoon all-purpose flour or cornstarch

-

1 teaspoon fresh lemon zest

-

2 tablespoons fresh lemon juice

PREPARATION

1. Combine crust ingredients. Pat into a 7-inch springform pan.
2. Beat cream cheese and sugar together until smooth and creamy; beat in eggs and continue beating on medium speed of a hand-held electric mixer for about 3 minutes.
3. Beat in remaining ingredients and continue beating for about 1 minute.
4. Pour batter into the prepared crust.
5. Place the cheesecake on a rack in the Crock Pot (crumpled foil can be used to form a rack).
6. Cover and cook on high for 2 1/2 to 3 hours.
7. Let the finished cheesecake stand in the covered pot after turning it off for about an hour or 2, until cool enough to handle.
8. Cool thoroughly before removing pan sides. Chill in the refrigerator before serving, and refrigerate any leftovers.

Orange Peanut Baked Apples

INGREDIENTS

-

6 cooking apples

-

1/2 cup raisins

-

3 tablespoons all-purpose flour

-

1/3 cup granulated sugar

-

1/2 teaspoon ground cinnamon

-

1/8 teaspoon salt

-

1 teaspoon finely grated orange peel

-

2 tablespoons peanut butter

-

2 tablespoons butter

-

1/4 cup chopped roasted peanuts

-

2/3 cup water

-

2/3 cup orange juice

- cream (optional)

PREPARATION

1. Wash apples and core. Peel apples about a third of the way down from stem end. Fill hollowed out center with raisins; set apples in crockpot, stacking if necessary. Combine flour, sugar, cinnamon, salt, orange peel, peanut butter and butter until crumbly. Add peanuts and sprinkle over apples. Mix water and orange juice; pour around the apples. Cover crockpot and cook on low 7 to 9 hours, until apples are tender.
2. Serve warm, plain or with heavy cream.
3. Makes 6 servings

Maggie's Baked Apples

INGREDIENTS

- 7 or 8 medium apples, cored

- Clementine orange sections

- raisins

- cinnamon

PREPARATION

1. Stuff apples with orange sections, raisins, and cinnamon; pile them in the Crock Pot. Add 1/4 cup water. Cover and cook on low most of the day, about 7 to 9 hours.
2. Maggie notes the apples shrunk a bit, but held up very well.

Mint Butter Wafers

INGREDIENTS

- 2 T. butter

- 1/4 C. milk

- 1 pkg. white frosting mix (dry)

- 3 drops peppermint flavoring

PREPARATION

1. Melt butter and milk together in a covered slow cooker on HIGH setting. Stir in frosting mix and cook 1 to 2 minutes longer. Add flavoring. Turn to low and drop by teaspoonfuls onto waxed paper.
2. Makes 5 dozen.

Peanut Butter-Chocolate Cheesecake

INGREDIENTS

-

Crust:

-

1 cup chocolate or regular graham cracker crumbs

-

2 tablespoons brown sugar

-

3 tablespoons melted butter

-

Filling:

-

12 oz cream cheese, room temperature

-

2/3 cup brown sugar

-

2 large eggs

-

1/3 cup creamy peanut butter

-

1 tablespoon all-purpose flour

-

1/2 teaspoon vanilla

-

1/2 cup chocolate chips, melted (semisweet or milk chocolate)

PREPARATION

1. Combine crumbs with 2 tablespoons of brown sugar; mix in melted butter until well moistened. Pat into a 7-inch springform pan.
2. In a medium-sized mixing bowl, with an electric mixer, cream together the cream cheese and 2/3 cup brown sugar. Add eggs and beat on medium speed for about 2 minutes. Add peanut butter, flour, and vanilla; beat about 2 more minutes.
3. Pour all but about 1/2 cup of the batter into the prepared pan.
4. Combine the melted chocolate chips with the remaining batter and pour on top of the batter in the pan.
5. Cut the chocolate batter in gently with a knife to make a swirling pattern, without disturbing the crust.
6. Place on a rack or aluminum foil ring (to keep the pan off the bottom of the pot) in the crockery cooker.
7. Cover and cook on high for 2 1/2 hours. Turn heat off and leave for about 1 1/2 to 2 hours, until cooled enough to remove.
8. Cool completely before removing from pan.
9. Chill before serving, and store leftovers in the refrigerator.

Oven: Bake at 325° F about 45 minutes to 1 hour, then turn the oven off and let it cool in the oven for about 4 hours.

Praline Cheesecake

INGREDIENTS

-

Crust:

-

1 cup graham cracker crumbs

-

1/4 cup finely chopped pecans

-

2 tablespoons brown sugar

-

3 tablespoons melted butter

Filling:

-

16 ounces cream cheese, room temperature

-

3/4 cup brown sugar

-

2 large eggs

-

1/4 cup whipping cream

-

1 teaspoon vanilla extract

-

1 tablespoon flour

PREPARATION

1. Combine crumbs and nuts with brown sugar; mix in melted butter until well moistened. Pat into a 7-inch springform pan.
2. Beat cream cheese and sugar together until smooth. Add the eggs, cream, vanilla, and flour; beat for 3 to 4 minutes at medium speed of a hand-held electric mixer. Pour into the prepared crust and place on a rack or ring of aluminum foil (to keep it off the bottom of the pot) in a 5 to 6-quart Crock Pot (large enough to fit the springform pan).
3. Cover and cook on high for 2 1/2 to 3 hours. Turn off and leave for 1 to 2 hours, until cool enough to remove.
4. Cool completely and remove the sides of the pan.
5. Garnish with pecan halves if desired.
6. Chill before serving, and store leftovers in the refrigerator.

Oven: Bake at 325° F about 45 minutes to 1 hour, then turn the oven off and let it cool in the oven for about 4 hours.

Pudding Cake
INGREDIENTS

-

1 cup flour

-

1/2 cup sugar

-

1/2 cup coarsely chopped pecans

-

1/4 cup unsweetened cocoa

-

2 teaspoons baking powder

-

1/2 teaspoon salt

-

1/2 cup milk

-

1/4 cup oil

-

1 teaspoon vanilla extract

-

1 cup boiling water

-

1/2 cup chocolate syrup

-

whipped cream or ice cream

PREPARATION

1. In mixing bowl, combine first 6 ingredients; stir in milk, oil and vanilla. Pour batter into 6-cup greased mold or similar container (make sure this will fit in your crockpot). Mix boiling water with chocolate syrup; pour over batter. Place small trivet, foil ring, or band from canning jar in bottom of cooker; add 2 cups warm water to the crockpot. Place mold in crockpot and cover with 4 layers of paper towels.
2. Cover crockpot and cook on high 3 to 4 hours.
3. Serve warm with heavy cream or ice cream.

Pumpkin Job

INGREDIENTS

- 1 can pumpkin puree (15 ounces)

- 1 scant tablespoon pumpkin pie spice

- 2 teaspoons vanilla

- 1 can evaporated milk (12 ounces)

- 3/4 cup sugar

- 1/2 cup biscuit mix

- 2 tablespoons butter

- 2 eggs

PREPARATION

1. Spray the slow cooker crock with non-stick spray or lightly oil the inside.
2. Combine all ingredients in a mixing bowl. Using an electric hand-held mixer at low to medium speed, beat ingredients together until smooth.
3. Pour the mixture into the prepared crockpot.
4. Cover and cook on Low 6 to 8 hours, or cook on High 3 to 4 hours.
5. Spoon into cups and top with whipped topping or a lightly spiced whipped cream.
6. Serves 6.

Pumpkin Tea Bread

INGREDIENTS

- 1/2 cup vegetable oil

- 1/2 cup granulated sugar

- 1/2 cup light or dark brown sugar, firmly packed

- 2 large eggs, beaten

- 1 cup canned pumpkin puree

- 1 1/2 cups sifted flour

- 1/2 teaspoon salt

- 1/2 teaspoon cinnamon

- 1/2 teaspoon nutmeg

- 1 teaspoon baking soda

- 1 cup chopped pecans or walnuts

PREPARATION

1. In mixing bowl, combine oil with granulated and brown sugars; blend well. Stir in beaten eggs and pumpkin puree. Sift dry ingredients together; stir into pumpkin mixture then fold in chopped nuts. Pour batter into greased and floured 1 lb. 10 oz. coffee can (make sure it will fit in your crockpot with cover on) or use baking dish which holds batter and fits in your crockpot. Place can in crockpot.

2. Cover top of can with 8 paper towels; place lid on crockpot. Bake on HIGH for 2 1/2 to 3 1/2 hours. Do not lift lid until the cake has cooked at least 2 hours.

Rhubarb Bake

INGREDIENTS

- 2 cups fresh sliced rhubarb

- 3/4 cup granulated sugar

- 1 cinnamon stick

- 1 teaspoon grated lemon peel

- 1/4 cup butter

- 1/3 cup flour

- 1/3 cup sugar

PREPARATION

1. Combine rhubarb with 3/4 cup sugar, cinnamon, and lemon peel in cooker. Cover and cook on LOW for 3 to 4 hours. Remove cinnamon. Spoon the rhubarb into baking dish. Combine remaining ingredients until crumbly and sprinkle over rhubarb. Bake at 400° for 20 to 25 minutes, until topping is nicely browned. Serve with whipped topping or ice cream.
2. Serves 4 to 6.

Rich Brownies in a Nut Crust

INGREDIENTS

- 1/4 cup melted butter

- 1 cup chopped pecans

- 1 family-size package brownie mix (about 20 to 23 ounces), along with ingredients for preparation

PREPARATION

1. Pour melted butter into 2-pound coffee can; swirl to coat bottom and sides well. Sprinkle with half of the chopped pecans. Mix brownies according to the package directions, stirring in remaining chopped pecans. Pour batter into the coffee can. Place can in slow cooker. Cover top of can with 8 paper towels. Cover and bake on HIGH for 3 hours. Do not check or remove cover until 45 to 60 minutes. Remove can; discard paper towels.
2. Let stand 5 minutes. Unmold and serve while warm, if desired.

Ricotta Amaretto Cheesecake

INGREDIENTS

-

Crust:

-

1 cup vanilla wafer crumbs (about 21 to 23 cookies)

-

1 tablespoon sugar

-

1/8 teaspoon almond extract

-

3 tablespoons melted butter

-

Filling:

-

15 ounces light ricotta cheese

-

8 ounces cream cheese, softened

-

2/3 cup sugar

-

3 large eggs plus 1 egg yolk

-

1/4 cup Amaretto liqueur

-

2 tablespoons all-purpose flour

- 1/4 teaspoon almond extract

- 1/2 teaspoon vanilla extract

PREPARATION

1. Combine crust ingredients well; pat into a 7-inch springform pan.
2. Beat sugar into the cheeses; add eggs; beat for 2 to 3 minutes on medium speed of an electric hand-held mixer. Add remaining filling ingredients and beat about 2 minutes more. Pour into prepared crust.
3. Place the cheesecake on a rack in the Crock-Pot (or use a "ring" of crumpled aluminum foil to keep it off the bottom of the pot). Cover and cook the cheesecake on high for 2 1/2 to 3 hours.
4. Let stand in the covered pot (after turning it off) for about 1 to 2 hours, until cool enough to handle.
5. Cool thoroughly before removing pan sides.
6. Chill before serving; store leftovers in the refrigerator.

Oven: Bake at 325° F about 45 minutes to 1 hour, then turn the oven off and let it cool in the oven for about 4 hours.

Simple Slow Cooker Apple Dessert

INGREDIENTS

-

4 large apples, peeled, cored, quartered

-

1/2 cup light brown sugar

-

2 cups apple cider

-

2 cups water

-

2 cinnamon sticks or about 1 teaspoon ground cinnamon

-

3 tablespoons butter, cut in small pieces

-

1 tablespoon cornstarch mixed with 1 tablespoon cold water

-

1 teaspoon vanilla extract

PREPARATION

1. Put the apples in the slow cooker insert.
2. In a bowl, combine the brown sugar, cider, water, cinnamon sticks or cinnamon, and butter. Pour over the apples.
3. Cover and cook on HIGH for 2 to 2 1/2 hours, or until the apples are tender, stirring 2 or 3 times throughout the cooking.
4. Pour the juices into a saucepan and bring to a boil on the stovetop. Boil, stirring occasionally, for 8 to 10 minutes. Reduce heat to a simmer.
5. Combine the cornstarch and cold water and blend well. Stir into the simmering juices. Continue cooking, stirring constantly, until thickened. Stir in the vanilla.
6. Serve the apples with the cider sauce.
7. Serves 4.

Slow Cooker Breakfast Cobbler

INGREDIENTS

- 4 medium-sized apples, peeled, cored, and sliced

- 1/4 cup honey

- 1 teaspoon ground cinnamon

- 2 tablespoons melted butter

- 2 cups granola cereal, your favorite

PREPARATION

1. Place apples in buttered slow cooker; Combine remaining ingredients and sprinkle over apples. Cover and cook on LOW 7 to 9 hours or on HIGH 3 to 4 hours. Serve with cream or ice cream
2. Serves 4.

Slow Cooked Fruit Compote With Cinnamon

INGREDIENTS

*

1 can (approx. 15 ounces) sliced peaches

*

1 can (approx. 15 ounces) dark red cherries

*

1 can (approx. 15 ounces) sliced pears

*

1 can (approx. 15 ounces) apricot halves

*

4 tablespoons light brown sugar, packed

*

4 tablespoons frozen orange juice concentrate or regular orange juice

*

1/2 teaspoon cinnamon

PREPARATION

1. Drain fruits well. Put fruits in slow cooker insert with brown sugar, orange juice concentrate, and cinnamon. Stir gently, cover, and cook on LOW for 3 to 5 hours.
2. Serves 6 to 8.

Slow Cooker Orange Cinnamon Bread Pudding

INGREDIENTS

-

6 slices bread, about 6 ounces, torn into small pieces

-

1/2 cup golden or dark raisins

-

1 can (12 ounces) evaporated milk

-

4 large eggs

-

2 tablespoons melted butter

-

6 ounces orange juice concentrate

-

4 large eggs

-

1 cup sugar

-

1/2 teaspoon ground cinnamon

-

1 tablespoon vanilla extract

PREPARATION

1. Generously butter a 1 1/2-quart souffle dish or 7-cup Pyrex glass straight-sided container/casserole.
2. Put bread and raisins in a large bowl. Set aside.
3. In another bowl, whisk milk and eggs with melted butter, orange juice concentrate, sugar, cinnamon, and vanilla; pour over the bread mixture and blend well.
4. Pour into prepared bowl/casserole.
5. Tear off a 16-inch length of foil and fold lengthwise twice to form a sturdy lift for the finished pudding.
6. Fit the foil in the slow cooker, letting the ends lay outside. Pour about 1 cup of very hot water into the crockpot. Place the bread pudding in the crockery, arrange foil "handles" to the inside and cover the pot.
7. Cook on HIGH for 2 1/2 hours. Using pot holders, gently use the "handles" to lift the dish up out of the pot so that you can get a grip on the outside of the dish. Place on a rack to cool slightly.
8. Serve warm with vanilla sauce or an orange sauce.

Slow Cooker Rice Pudding With Mixed Berries

INGREDIENTS

- 1 package (6 ounces) dried cranberries

- 1 package (4 ounces) dried blueberries

- 1 can (12 ounces) evaporated milk

- 1 1/2 cups water

- 8 ounces frozen orange juice concentrate

- 3/4 cup sugar

- 1 cup heavy cream

- Dash salt

- 1/4 teaspoon ground cinnamon

- 1 cup short-grain Arborio rice

PREPARATION

1. Spray the inside of the crockery insert with nonstick cooking spray.
2. Combine all ingredients and pour into the slow cooker.
3. Cover and cook on LOW for 4 to 5 hours or on HIGH for 2 to 2 1/2 hours, or until rice is tender and mixture has thickened.
4. Stir the mixture about halfway through the cooking time and shortly before it's done.
5. 6 Servings

Spoon Peaches

INGREDIENTS

-

1/4 cup granulated sugar

-

1/2 cup brown sugar

-

3/4 cup biscuit mix

-

2 eggs, beaten

-

2 teaspoons vanilla

-

2 teaspoons melted butter

-

2/3 cup evaporated milk

-

2 cups peach slices, mashed

-

1 scant teaspoon cinnamon

PREPARATION

1. Spray slow cooker with non-stick cooking spray. Combine sugars and the biscuit mix. Stir in eggs and vanilla. blend in the melted butter and milk. Add peaches and cinnamon. Pour into slow cooker/Crock Pot. Cook on low for 6 to 8 hours.

Steamed Pumpkin-Date Pudding

INGREDIENTS

- 1 cup brown sugar

- 1/2 cup shortening

- 2 eggs, separated

- 1 3/4 cups all-purpose flour

- 1 teaspoon salt

- 1 teaspoon baking soda

- 1 teaspoon baking powder

- 1 teaspoon ground cinnamon

- 1 teaspoon nutmeg

- 1 teaspoon ground ginger

- 1 16 oz can pumpkin or 1 1/2 cups fresh cooked and pureed pumpkin

- 1/4 cup evaporated milk

- 1 cup chopped dates

- 1/2 cup chopped pecans

PREPARATION

1. Cream brown sugar and shortening. Add egg yolks, beating well. Mix flour, salt, butter, baking powder, baking soda, cinnamon, nutmeg, and ginger together and beat in alternately with pumpkin and milk. Fold in dates and nuts. Beat egg whites until they hold stiff peaks and gently fold into batter. Put mixture into a well-oiled or buttered 6-cup mold or souffle dish. Place a small trivet in a Crock Pot large enough for the souffle dish, and add about 1/2 to 3/4-inch of water to the Crock Pot.

2. If you don't have a trivet, make a ring of foil just thick enough to keep the souffle dish out of the water. Cut a round of wax paper to fit the top of the souffle dish and lightly grease it so batter will not stick as it rises, then wrap well with aluminum foil. Put in Crock Pot and cook on LOW for 4 to 5 hours.

Stewed Fruits

INGREDIENTS

- 16 ounces prunes, pitted

- 8 ounces dried apricots

- 8 ounces dried pears

- 3 cups water

- 1/2 cup sugar

- 1/2 vanilla bean or 1/2 teaspoon vanilla

- 1 teaspoon finely grated lemon zest

- 2 tablespoons fresh lemon juice

PREPARATION

1. Combine all ingredients together in the Crock Pot and cook on low until the fruit is tender, 6 to 8 hours.
2. Serve warm or at room temperature.
3. Yield: 6 to 8 servings.

Strawberry-Rhubarb Cobbler

INGREDIENTS

- 2 1/2 cups sliced rhubarb

- 1 1/2 cups sliced strawberries

- 3/4 cup sugar

- 1/2 cup water

- 2 teaspoons lemon juice

- 2 tablespoons cornstarch mixed with just enough cold water to make a smooth paste

- 1 c. + 1 tbsp. flour (or use self-rising flour and omit baking powder)

- 3 tbsp. sugar

- 1 1/2 tsp. baking powder

- 1/4 tsp. salt

- 1/4 cup cold butter

- 1/2 cup milk or half & half

PREPARATION

1. Combine fruit, sugar, water, and lemon juice in slow cooker/Crock Pot. Cover and cook on low 4 to 5 hours. Mix cornstarch with a little cold water and add to mixture. Turn to high. Blend dry ingredients. Cut butter in until mixture is grainy; mix milk in until just moistened. Drop small amounts over fruit mixture.
2. Cover and cook for about 1 hour on high.

Streusel Pound Cake

INGREDIENTS

- 1 box pound cake mix, 16 ounces

- 1/4 cup light brown sugar, firmly packed

- 1 tablespoon all-purpose flour

- 1/4 cup finely chopped pecans

- 1 teaspoon ground cinnamon

- 2 teaspoons butter

PREPARATION

1. Mix cake mix according to package directions. Pour batter into well greased and floured 2 pound coffee tin (make sure it will fit in your crockpot with cover) or baking dish which holds batter and fits in your crockpot. Combine sugar, flour, nuts, cinnamon, and butter; sprinkle over cake batter. Place can in slow cooker. Cover top of can with 8 layers of paper towels. Cover slow cooker and bake on high for 3 to 4 hours.

Triple Chocolate Pudding Cake

INGREDIENTS

-

1 package chocolate cake mix (2-layer size)

-

2 cups sour cream

-

1 package instant chocolate pudding (any size)

-

1 cup semisweet chocolate chips

-

3/4 cup vegetable oil•

-

4 large eggs

-

1 cup water

PREPARATION

1. Spray crock pot with non-stick spray.
2. Mix all ingredients together in a bowl until well blended; transfer to the slow cooker.
3. Cover and cook on LOW for 6 to 8 hours. Do not lift the lid.
4. Serve with ice cream.

Warm Spiced Fruit

INGREDIENTS

- 1 large can (28 to 29 ounces) peach slices, drained (28 to 29 ounces)

- 1 can pineapple tidbits with natural juices, undrained (8 to 16 ounces)

- 1 large can (28 to 29 ounces) pear slices, drained (28 to 29 ounces)

- 1 can (15 ounces) mixed chunky fruit

- maraschino cherries, drained, about 1/2 cup, or as desired

- 1 tablespoon cornstarch

- 1 1/2 teaspoons ground cinnamon

- 1 teaspoon ground nutmeg

- 1/2 cup brown sugar

- 4 tablespoons butter

PREPARATION

1. Combine all ingredients in the slow cooker; stir gently.
2. Cover and cook on LOW for about 4 to 6 hours or on HIGH for 2 to 3 hours. Serve with heavy cream or a dollop of sour cream, if desired.
3. Serves 8.

Zucchini Bread

INGREDIENTS

- 2 large eggs

- 2/3 cup vegetable oil

- 1 1/4 cup sugar

- 1 1/3 cups zucchini, peeled and grated

- 1 tablespoon vanilla extract

- 2 cups all-purpose flour

- 1/4 teaspoon salt

- 1/2 teaspoon baking powder

- 1 1/2 teaspoons ground cinnamon

- 1/4 teaspoon ground nutmeg

- 1 cup chopped pecans or walnuts

PREPARATION

1. In mixing bowl with electric mixer, beat eggs until light and foamy. Add oil, sugar, grated zucchini and vanilla. Mix well.
2. Combine the dry ingredients in another bowl with nuts; stir well to blend. Stir into zucchini mixture and blend well.
3. Pour into a greased and floured 2 pound coffee can or 2 quart mold (whatever you use, make sure it fits in your slow cooker). Place in slow cooker.
4. Cover can or dish with 8 paper towels.
5. Cover and bake on HIGH for 3 to 4 hours.
6. Do not remove cover to check cake until it has cooked for 3 hours. Let stand 5 minutes before unmolding.

Beans with Tuna

INGREDIENTS

- 4 tablespoons olive oil

- 1 clove garlic, crushed

- 1 pound small white beans, soaked overnight drained

- 2 cups chopped tomatoes

- 2 6-1/2oz can white tuna in water, drained and flaked

- 2 sprigs basil, finely chopped, or 1 1/2 teaspoons dried basil

- salt and pepper, to taste\

PREPARATION

1. Saute garlic in oil until brown; discard garlic. Combine the garlic flavored oil with beans and 6 cups water (48 ounces) in crockpot. Cover and cook on high 2 hours. Turn heat to low, cover and cook 8 hours. Add remaining ingredients; cover and cook on high for 30 minutes.

Cheese 'n Pasta Delight (Tuna or Chicken)

INGREDIENTS

- 1 lb chicken tenders or chicken breasts, cubed

- 1 can (15 oz) tomatoes, diced

- 1 small can (6 oz) tomato paste

- 1 rib celery, sliced

- 1/4 cup chopped onion

- 1/2 cup chopped or shredded carrots, canned or cooked until slightly tender

- 1/2 tsp oregano

- 1/2 tsp salt

- 1/4 tsp pepper

- 1/2 tsp garlic powder

- pinch of sugar or other sweetener (optional or to taste)

PREPARATION

1. Combine all ingredients in slow cooker or crockpot. Cover and cook on low for 6 to 8 hours. Taste and adjust seasonings about 30 minutes before serving and add a little water to thin, if necessary. Serve this easy recipe for chicken pasta sauce over spaghetti, fettucine or other pasta.
2. This easy recipe with chicken serves 4.

Chicken and Sausage Gumbo With Shrimp

INGREDIENTS

- 3 tablespoons all-purpose flour

- 3 tablespoons oil

- 1/2 pound smoked sausage, cut into 1/2 inch slices

- 3/4 to 1 pound boneless chicken thighs, cut in bite-size pieces

- 1 1/2 to 2 cups frozen cut okra

- 1 cup chopped onion

- 1/2 cup chopped green bell pepper

- 3 cloves garlic, minced

- 1/4 teaspoon ground cayenne pepper, or to taste

- 1/4 teaspoon ground black pepper

- 1 can (14.5 ounces) diced tomatoes, undrained

- 1 cup frozen medium shrimp, cleaned and cooked

• 1 1/2 cups uncooked regular long-grain white rice

•

3 cups chicken broth or water (updated 9/07)

PREPARATION

1. In small saucepan, combine flour and oil; mix well. Cook, stirring constantly, over medium-high heat for 5 minutes. Reduce heat to medium-low; cook, stirring constantly, about 8 to 12 minutes or until mixture turns a light reddish brown.
2. Place flour and oil mixture in 3 1/2 to 4-quart slow cooker insert. Add all remaining ingredients except shrimp, rice, and broth or water; stir well.
3. Cover and cook on LOW for 7 to 9 hours.
4. Add the cooked shrimp to the gumbo; mix well.
5. Cover and continue to cook on LOW for 20 minutes longer. Meanwhile, cook rice in the broth or water following package directions.
6. Serve gumbo over the hot cooked rice along with cornbread or biscuits.
7. Serves 6 to 8.

Chicken and Shrimp

INGREDIENTS

- 2 pounds chicken, boneless thighs and breasts, skin removed, cut in chunks

- 2 tablespoons of extra virgin olive oil

- 1 cup chopped onion

- 2 cloves garlic, minced

- 1/4 cup parsley, minced

- 1/2 cup white wine

- 1 large can (15 ounces) tomato sauce

- 1 teaspoon dried leaf basil

- 1 pound uncooked shrimp, peeled and deveined

- salt and freshly ground black pepper, to taste

- 1 pound fettuccine, linguine, or spaghetti

PREPARATION

1. In a large skillet or sauté pan over medium heat, heat the olive oil. Add the chicken chunks and cook, stirring, until lightly browned. Remove chicken to slow cooker.
2. Add a little more oil to the pan and sauté the onion, garlic, and parsley for about 1 minute. Remove from heat and stir in the wine, tomato sauce, and dried basil. Pour the mixture over chicken in slow cooker.
3. Cover and cook on LOW for 4 to 5 hours.
4. Stir in shrimp, cover, and cook on LOW for about 1 hour longer.
5. Season with salt and freshly ground black pepper, to taste.
6. Just before the dish is done, cook the pasta in boiling salted water as directed on the package.

Citrus Fish - Crockpot

INGREDIENTS

*

1 1/2 pounds fish fillets

*

salt and pepper to taste

*

1/2 cup chopped onion

*

5 tablespoons chopped fresh parsley

*

1 tablespoon vegetable oil

*

2 teaspoons grated lemon rind

*

2 teaspoons grated orange rind

*

Orange and lemon slices, for garnish

*

parsley sprigs, for garnish

PREPARATION

1. Butter slow cooker; sprinkle fish fillets with salt and pepper. Place fish in crockpot. Put onion, parsley, grated orange and lemon rind, and oil over fish. Cover and cook on LOW for 1 1/2 hours.
2. Serve garnished with orange and lemon slices and sprigs of fresh parsley.

Crockpot Clam Chowder

INGREDIENTS

- 4 (6 1/2 oz.) cans minced clams with juice

- 1/2 lb. salt pork or bacon, diced

- 1 cup chopped onion

- 6 to 8 medium potatoes, peeled and cubed

- 3 cups water

- 3 1/2 teaspoons salt

- 1/4 teaspoon pepper

- 4 cups half and half cream or milk

- 3 to 4 tbsp. cornstarch

- chopped fresh parsley, for garnish

PREPARATION

1.   Cut clams into bite-sized pieces if necessary.
2.   In skillet, saute salt pork or bacon and onion until golden brown; drain. Put into slow cooker with clams.
3.   Add all remaining ingredients, except milk, cornstarch, and parsley.
4.   Cover and cook on high 3 to 4 hours or until vegetables are tender.
5.   During the last hour of cooking, combine 1 cup of milk or cream with the cornstarch. Add cornstarch mixture and the remaining milk or cream and stir well; heat through.
6.   Top each serving with a little chopped parsley and serve with crackers or crusty French bread.

Crockpot Jambalaya

INGREDIENTS

- 1 pound chicken breasts or tenders, boneless, cut in 1-inch cubes

- 8 to 12 ounces smoked sausage, sliced

- 1/2 cup chopped onion

- 1 green bell pepper, chopped

- 1 large can (28 ounces) crushed tomatoes

- 1 cup chicken broth

- 1/2 cup dry white wine

- 2 teaspoons dried leaf oregano

- 2 teaspoons dried parsley

- 2 teaspoons Cajun seasoning

- 1 teaspoon cayenne pepper

- 1 pound shrimp, cooked

- 2 cups long grain rice, cooked

PREPARATION

1. Combine chicken, sausage, chopped bell pepper, and chopped onion in slow cooker. Add tomatoes, chicken broth, wine, oregano, parsley, Cajun seasoning, and pepper; stir gently.
2. Cover and cook on LOW for 6 to 8 hours, or on HIGH for 3 to 4 hours.
3. About 30 to 30 minutes before eating, add cooked shrimp and hot cooked rice; heat thoroughly.
4. Serves 8.

www.ingramcontent.com/pod-product-compliance
Lightning Source LLC
Chambersburg PA
CBHW051056050726
47592CB00002B/555